treasures
of the
transformed
life

treasures
of the
transformed
life

satisfying your soul's thirst for more

JOHN ED MATHISON

Abingdon Press
Nashville

TREASURES OF THE TRANSFORMED LIFE
SATISFYING YOUR SOUL'S THIRST FOR MORE

Cover and page design by Joey McNair.
Art by Steve Cohen/FoodPix/Jupiterimages.

Library of Congress Cataloging-in-Publication Data

Mathison, John Ed, 1939–
   Treasures of the transformed life : satisfying your soul's thirst for more / John Ed Mathison.
       p. cm.
   ISBN 0-687-33445-4 (binding: pbk. : alk. paper)
   1. Spiritual formation. 2. Spiritual life--Christianity. 3. Christian life. I. Title.

   BV4511.M38 2006
   248.4'876--dc22

                          2006012853

ISBN–13: 978-0-687-33445-2
ISBN–10: 0-687-33445-4

06   07   08   09   10   11   12   13   14   15   10   9   8   7   6   5   4   3   2

MANUFACTURED IN THE UNITED STATES OF AMERICA

contents

contents

acknowledgments

This book would never have been written without the assistance, support, and encouragement of many, many people. Chief among them are the members of Frazer Memorial United Methodist Church, whom I have served as pastor for more than thirty-four years. In fact, a good deal of the book started life as sermons written expressly for my Frazer family. I have been—and continue to be—mightily blessed to be part of such a wonderful group of believers. Thank you each and every one!

The Frazer staff have all contributed to this material, as they have all added to my life and what I know and write about. In particular, I would like to thank a few individuals on the Frazer staff for their contributions and support. John Schmidt, my ministry partner, helped shape many of the messages and approaches referenced in this book. Mary Lou Windham has been Frazer's talented director of stewardship for more than twenty-two years. While this book isn't about Frazer's stewardship program, what we learned together in experimenting with different strategies and approaches did provide valuable insight. My assistant, Linda Poole, never fails to keep me on track and wonderfully makes my life easier. My wonderful wife, Lynn, provides insight, heart, and joy, as do our incredible children and grandchildren.

The leadership at Abingdon Press saw the need for this book and have worked hard to help it impact lives. Abingdon's development partner, Providence House Publishers, led by Andrew Miller, and his staff, including Nancy Wise, Mark Jacobs, Holly Jones, Joey McNair, Melissa Istre, and Tammy Spurlock, believed in the power of this work and in what God will do with it. We all have worked closely together for many months, selecting themes, shaping content, designing the resources and packaging, and developing marketing plans for this transforming study. I'd also like to add a very special thank you to Fiona Soltes, for her vision, grace, creativity, and ability to be led by the Holy Spirit on this project.

All glory and honor always goes to our Lord and Savior Jesus Christ, whose presence has been felt continuously throughout the development process. He is truly "the author and finisher" of all things. We are all privileged to be in his almighty service.

treasures
of the
transformed
life

introduction

Have you ever wanted something so much that you'd do anything to get it? Whether it was a job, a goal, or even a relationship, something compelled you. And you knew that whatever it took to achieve it, it would be worthwhile.

A merchant once felt the same way. He had his eyes set on a pearl, a single, solitary, beautiful pearl, and according to the Bible story in Matthew 13:45–46, he sold everything he had so he could buy it. Imagine that. Everything he owned. Now, we're not told what that merchant did with the pearl once he possessed it. But we do know a couple of things: We know that he was in the process of actively looking when he came across it, and we know that it represents the kingdom of Heaven.

So many of us spend time looking for things, striving for goals, and hoping for something better. I understand, because I've been there. Then one day, I found that pearl of great price myself, and nothing was ever the same again.

Today, I'm dedicated to helping other people find it, and to helping them deepen their understanding of how truly beautiful that pearl can be. At my church in Montgomery, Alabama, one way we do that is by diving into the depths of God and the Bible together. For several years, the entire church has taken part in a six-week study that's integrated through Sunday school classes, small groups, communications, and teaching. We've found that this process results in tremendous personal growth and satisfaction.

These studies also draw us closer as a congregation. People always like to feel as if we are part of a team, part of something bigger than ourselves. I don't simply mean being part of a large-size church. No, I mean that something bigger that is relationship with God, deeper understanding of self, and finding our place in the Kingdom.

During this time, we focus on commitment and on really applying the concepts of the Bible to our lives. The Bible, after all, is something like a sports playbook or a roadmap on a long journey; its timeless truths offer perspective, guidance, and the foundation on which our whole faith system rests.

I was approached a year or so ago to consider sharing with others beyond our congregation what we've learned (and I include myself in that learning). I don't mind telling you that I was humbled, surprised, and then, excited, about the request. You hold the result in your hands.

This book and study are for you, and about you. As you read and consider this content, I believe you'll learn a little and grow a lot—no matter where you are in your spiritual walk. At the end of each day's lesson, you'll find questions to consider. Use them as an opportunity to prayerfully review where you are in regard to each topic. Ask God to help you answer the questions honestly, and you just might be surprised what you discover about yourself. You don't even have to read the book as part of a congregation-wide study to become richer, although my experience has been that a church-wide study creates powerful, unified, fulfilling results.

I know that in every congregation, and in every group of people in general, there are people at different stages. This study is designed to have treasure for everyone at every stage. You might already consider yourself like that merchant, in search of something worthwhile. Or this might be the first time you've thought and prayed about some of the things in this book. It doesn't matter. The treasure is there for everyone. The truth is, you have a chance to be like the oyster and discover that you already have that pearl of great price within you.

There's a funny thing about pearls, you know: They grow better in deep water. So go ahead. Jump in.

You just might be surprised at how refreshing it can be.

part I

priming
the pump

chapter 1

the need for more

The next time you're in a restaurant, pay attention to whether the server brings you a glass of water. It used to be that it was standard. You sat down, you got a glass of water, and the server would ask if you'd like anything else to drink.

You'll probably still see two glasses on the table at more formal places, one for water and one for something else; in most restaurants, though, it seems to be either or. There are so many other choices on the menu. You can have a soft drink, lemonade, tea, maybe even fruit tea, coffee, you name it. There are all sorts of ways to satisfy your thirst.

Now, we all know that nothing is quite as good for us as pure water. It helps the body better do its job. It helps wash the junk out, it helps maintain peace in the body's functions, and it makes sure all the essential nutrients get to where they're supposed to go. That's why doctors tell us to drink so much of it every day.

But you know how it is. Sometimes you look at that glass and think, *Nothing special about that.* Sometimes it looks plain.

Ordinary. You begin to think about how much you'd rather have something else. Something that looks really good and tasty.

We can keep our eyes on the things that look good and tasty on the outside. We can try to satisfy our thirst with coffee, soft drinks, maybe even beer or wine. But all the while, something deep within us is still crying out for the real deal—good, pure water. Nothing will feel right until we get it.

That doesn't just apply to what we drink. Sometimes we can get thirsty in life, too. Sometimes we begin wondering if there's really more to it. If it's really possible to be happier, more content, more satisfied. . . . Ever been there?

the thirst within

Psychologists tell us that most people in America today are unsatisfied. They don't like their jobs. They don't like where they live. Or others don't like the weather. They don't like their health. In general, they just don't like their lives. They may feel that things are okay as they are. Maybe they don't know anyone who's happier, less stressed, or less busy; so they figure that's just how life is supposed to be. Yet, they don't think anything can change. Someone asks them—or us—how things are, and we reply, "Fine"—even if everything really isn't and we want more out of our days on this earth.

Consider this story about a little girl who sat down to eat her lunch. There was a peanut butter sandwich and a glass of milk on the table, but she didn't touch any of it. About two hours later, she went to her mother and said, "I don't feel good." The mother asked what was wrong, and she replied, "I've got a stomachache."

At that point, the mother looked over and noticed that the sandwich and the glass of milk were still sitting there. So she said, "Honey, your stomach hurts because it's empty. You need to put something in it. Eat your lunch and you'll feel better."

About that time, the preacher stopped by the house to discuss some church business. As they were talking, he said,

"You know, I've had a headache all day long." The little girl looked at him and said, "I know why. It's because your head's empty. If you put something in it, it wouldn't be so bad."

Do you know when the great pain in life comes? It comes when we're empty. It might not be our stomachs or our heads, but it might be our hearts. If your heart and life are empty, that's the worst kind of pain there is.

We get to this point in different ways. Sometimes we come up empty because we realize that we have a thirst deep down inside, but we try to satisfy it with other people, jobs, material things, nice houses and cars, or relationships. They all look good for a while, but that kind of fulfillment never really lasts. It's kind of like drinking a big cup of coffee. It warms us for a while, and the caffeine might even boost our spirits and make us feel pretty good. Sooner or later, however, that all wears off, and we're back in search of another cup.

> None are so empty as those who
> are full of themselves.
>
> **—Benjamin Whichcote**

Sometimes we come up empty because we've been disappointed. Maybe we're burned out. Maybe we've developed a "been there, done that" mentality, and talked ourselves into believing that the way things are is as good as they'll ever get. Perhaps we just don't know any better. Nobody ever told us the truth about life, so we think our happiness depends entirely upon us, according to what we can accomplish.

If you've ever felt that way, I've got some good news for you. There really is more, and it's ours for the asking. It really is possible to live a full life, one in which you look forward to waking up each morning, one full of joy, faith, and strength.

delusions of self-sufficiency

I once read a story about a lady who went to work at a large mill, where her job was to sew. On her first day, the foreman said, "The most important thing you need to know is this: If your threads get tangled, call me and I'll fix them." He then pointed to a sign on the wall. There, right in front of her, was a reminder: "If your threads get tangled, call the foreman."

The lady sat down and began to sew. Eventually, her threads started to tangle. She thought, *I won't bother the foreman; he's too busy. I'll do it myself.* She tried to untangle the threads, but they just became more and more tangled. Before long, she really had a mess on her hands.

The foreman came by and said, "You didn't do what you were told, did you?"

She replied, "No. I wanted to do it myself." Then she added, "I want you to know that I did the best that I could."

The foreman responded, "No, you didn't. If you had done the best that you could, you would have called me."

Isn't that what's wrong with life most of the time? I know so many who are doing the best they can, but life is still getting all tangled up. And all they have to do—all any of us have to do—is call on the One who made our lives, who made the thread, the One who knows how to untangle it and put it all back together into something beautiful.

drink deeply

This is where it all comes together. The life that God has for us, the one he really intends for us to live, is a lot like that glass of water we talked about a moment ago. It's refreshing, it's good for us, and it satisfies our thirst in a way that absolutely nothing else can. But it's something we have to take in often, and we've got to drink it down deep.

Scientists have discovered that by the time we actually recognize we're thirsty, we've already begun down the path of dehydration. Many of us only drink a glass of water occasionally. As a result, we really only take in enough water to quench a dry throat, but never enough to recover all the water we've lost. We know we need something, but we can't quite put our fingers on it. Doctors have found that many times when we think we're hungry and go looking for food, we're actually just thirsty and don't know how to recognize our need.

The same principle applies to our relationship with God. We can get so caught up in life that we only talk to him occasionally. We often become so accustomed to our constant state of spiritual dehydration that we don't even know what we're thirsty for any more.

> **God is not what you imagine or what you think you understand. If you understand you have failed.**
> **—St. Augustine**

And yet, the Bible urges us to seek God. Isaiah 55:6 says, "Seek the LORD while you can find him. Call on him now while he is near." We are to seek—to intentionally devote all of our time, energy, and effort into going after God.

Consider this: Do you seek God? When you have a decision to make, do you seek his advice? When you need comfort, do you seek his presence?

That's where the abundant life is found. When we're willing to believe that there really is more to this life—and that God is the only One who can provide the way—all sorts of things begin to happen. He opens his arms to us and welcomes us as friends. He helps us forget the things in our past that we'd rather not remember. He takes all those threads we've managed to tangle up and begins weaving them together into a tapestry that we couldn't previously imagine.

satisfaction guaranteed

During the course of this study, we're going to take a closer look at the process of seeking God. Basically, we're giving a promise, and it works like this: If you give God more of yourself, he will give you more of himself. Along with this comes that sense of satisfaction, that overflowing abundance of joy and peace.

> A little faith will bring your soul to heaven, but a lot of faith will bring heaven to your soul.
>
> **—Author Unknown**

We'll look at what it really means to pray, and ways to make your prayer life rich, rewarding, and exciting. We'll talk about finding your place in the Body of Christ, and how to know that you're doing the things that you alone were created to do.

We're going to talk about building a relationship with the One who created you, and making sure that you're well positioned to receive everything that he has to offer.

This all begins with a recognition of thirst—even if you don't think you're thirsty—and a willingness to satisfy it in the only way that will last: With the pure goodness of being fully hydrated, and the understanding of where living water comes from.

So go ahead and raise your glass. It doesn't matter if you see it as half full or half empty—just as long as you see it.

dive in

- *For what am I thirsty?*
- *In what ways do I try to satisfy that thirst?*
- *How could God help?*

chapter 2

God really does care

I t was high noon, and the woman was at the well alone.

Theologians would tell us that she picked the time out of shame, knowing that she could avoid the stares and comments from the other disapproving women, the ones who knew she'd been married five times.

But that may not be the case. The woman wasn't one who was thirsty without realizing it. No, she very much needed a drink. She needed it so much that she was there in the heat of the day, when most others would have been resting out of the midday sun. She did what she thought she had to do.

We find this woman's compelling story in John 4:1–18. She encountered Jesus at the well, and he offered her living water—an opportunity to refresh her soul, receive cleansing from past sins, and bring to life places that she long felt were dead.

Sometimes this story is recounted with an emphasis on the fact that the woman was a Samaritan and that Jesus was a

Jew. As such, Jesus crossed traditional boundaries to reach out to her. Society well understood that Samaritans and Jews just didn't associate with each other.

If we stop there, we miss a richness that goes beyond the idea that Jesus simply loves everyone, regardless of gender, race, or background. We miss the idea that he met the woman right where she was. He actually went out of his way to meet her there in order to satisfy her thirst.

The woman could very well have been waiting for this opportunity. She probably wasn't just looking for a cup of cool water. She was also hoping for someone who would understand, someone who wouldn't judge her, someone who would be able to see beyond the things of which she wasn't proud to the person she knew she really could be.

searching souls

We've all been there. We were created with a thirst to be more than we are and more than the world thinks of us. We were created to live rich lives full of meaning and fulfillment.

Perhaps we're not there yet. If we choose to be, however, we can get a little closer every day.

Every one, though born of God
in an instant, yet undoubtedly
grows by slow degrees.

—John Wesley

Many of us have become complacent, maybe even bored, with the idea of living a life that glorifies God. Some may not even realize that their lives can be more satisfying with God. And there are also many like the Samaritan woman who are really thirsty. They may not have done the same things she had, but they're still going to the well, day after day, looking for something that will satisfy. Some may even be going the difficult way, carrying their shame just as she did, trying to avoid anyone who might judge them for wanting more, anyone who might talk about what they deserve.

Thank goodness for a little thing called grace. God extends that grace to us, no matter who we are, no matter what we've done. All we have to do is approach the well expectantly, and there he is, waiting to give us that stuff he calls "living water."

This living water comes through faith in Jesus. If you are thirsty, but have not yet hooked up to the everlasting spring, refer to the appendix (page 311), where will you find an explanation of how you can invite God's living water into your life.

a key element

The Bible has a lot of references to water. Consider, for instance, the parting of the Red Sea, a showing of God's power, strength, and willingness to protect his people; the floods that covered the earth, giving Noah the chance to declare his faith by building a boat when others said he was crazy; the time that Jesus washed the feet of his disciples, showing them a true model of humility; and Jesus' first miracle, turning water into wine.

But living water is something different. It wells up inside of us when we finally understand that we're not the ones who choose God. No, he's the One who chooses us. Remember, Jesus actually went out of his way to meet the Samaritan woman at the well. John 4:3–4 tells us that, on his way from Judea to Galilee, Jesus "had to" pass through Samaria. Jesus could have gone the way most other Jews would have, crossing the Jordan. But he didn't. He already knew that someone in Samaria needed what only he could give. He chose to make himself available.

That is how God operates. He makes himself available to meet us wherever we are. This is plainly stated in Isaiah 43:2–5.

> When you go through deep waters and great trouble, I will be with you. When you go through rivers of difficulty, you will not drown! When you walk through the fire of oppression, you will not be burned up; the flames will not consume you. For I am the LORD, your God, the Holy One of Israel, your Savior. . . . Do not be afraid, for I am with you.

taking the plunge

To really understand the concept of living water, it must be understood that the One who made you, God himself, is absolutely committed to you. Jesus reminds us in John 15:5 that he is the vine and we're the branches. As such, we will wither up and die without the life force, the living water, flowing directly from Jesus to us.

God created you to need that water, and to need him. You just have to go to the well to drink. There's nothing that God can't accomplish through a person who is connected to him. But understand this: It takes faith to get there, and it might not be faith in the way you currently understand it.

Author, philosopher, and theologian Elton Trueblood says that, "Faith is closer to courage than it is to intellectual assent," or belief. You just have to put your eyes on Jesus and trust that he'll get you where you need to go. We tend to think that faith is something you only believe with your mind. Trueblood points out that faith is also acting with your body. Some people believe something without ever actually doing anything about it. It takes courage to act on your beliefs.

Consider Peter in the boat with the other disciples. As the story goes in Matthew 14:22–36, he looked up to see Jesus coming across the lake to meet them. Jesus simply walked on the water to get to where they were. The disciples couldn't believe their eyes.

Peter did a bold thing: He decided to put Jesus to the test. Seeing Jesus approach, he said, "Lord, if it's really you, tell me to come to you by walking on water."

Jesus replied, "Come." When we try to put Jesus to the test, he often has a way of turning it around so we're the ones being tested. He gave Peter an invitation to take a risk, but the responsibility fell to Peter to make it happen.

Keep in mind that Peter was familiar with boats and was a fisherman. He'd crossed that lake thousands of times, always in a boat. He'd seen thousands of people on that lake, and each time they were safe in a boat. There was safety in the wood on the bottom of that boat, safety in what Peter had already experienced during his lifetime.

This was a new challenge, an opportunity to see if that water could really be as secure as the boat he'd been in all that time. He decided to go for it.

> ## Sometimes the biggest act of courage is a small one.
> ### —Lauren Raffo

Imagine the looks on the faces of the other disciples as Peter stepped onto the water. He didn't just stick one foot out and keep the other in the boat. Faith is never putting one foot out and checking it. Faith is a decision, a cutting off from where I am and stepping, with risk, into the place Jesus is inviting me. The *only* way to walk on water is to put both feet out there and trust Jesus. Faith involves letting go of every form of security, trusting God completely and without reservation.

As long as Peter kept his eyes on Jesus and continued walking toward him, he was able to do amazing things and experienced success. As soon as he started looking away, his success was jeopardized and he began to sink.

Remember what he did next. He cried out, "Save me, Lord!"

He probably wasn't slowly sinking in the water and saying that in a quiet voice. He was most likely kicking, and screaming, and splashing to avoid drowning.

lifeline

Have you ever been there and needed to cry out for help? Take comfort in the response of Jesus in verse 31: "Instantly Jesus reached out his hand and grabbed him." Jesus didn't say, "Well, I told you not to do that." He didn't say, "I'm busy right now, but I'll get to you when I can."

He responded *instantly*. Jesus was right there, knowing what Peter would need before Peter even knew he'd need it. Jesus will do the same for you.

dive in

- *If I met Jesus at the well, what could he reveal about my life that others may not know?*
- *Have I ever put Jesus to the test? How did he respond?*
- *What's my response when Jesus says, "Come"?*

What we are is God's gift to us.
What we become is our gift to God.

—Eleanor Powell

chapter 3
great expectations

God is committed to us: he's here for us, he encourages and loves us, and he satisfies the deepest desires of our hearts. Have you ever considered what kind of commitment God might expect from us in return?

A man came to me some time ago. He'd been active in the church, even been a leader in some things. That day, he admitted that he'd fooled people his entire life by trying to be a "good" Christian. He explained, "I've come to a point in my life that I just can't do it any more. I can't live with myself. I've got to either make a commitment that's real, or I'm going to forget about life completely."

We talked about it for awhile, and he ended up kneeling in my office. He prayed, "God, I want my commitment to be real, and I'm surrendering to you. I'm not going to try to fool people any more." That man is now a completely different person.

There's a well-known saying that "you can fool some of the people all of the time and all of the people some of the time."

There are two people that you can never fool—yourself and God. We can put on a good face and have a counterfeit faith of sorts in which we say and do the right things. Doing this, I can fool some people, but I can never fool myself, and I can never fool God.

the real deal

So if I profess to follow God, what kind of commitment does he expect from me? One that is real. Not one that's counterfeit, that merely looks good on the outside. The commitment must be genuine and authentic.

Do you know how bank tellers and others who handle money learn how to recognize counterfeit bills? They don't spend their time examining the fakes. Instead, they become so familiar with real money that anything else just won't do.

We can get that way in our relationship with God, too. We can grow to the point that we recognize his true hand in our lives and are so familiar with who he really is that we won't waste our time looking for something else to satisfy us. When we're truly committed to God, he becomes enough.

Commitment involves establishing priorities. Matthew 6:33 tells us to seek *first* God's kingdom, and *then* all things will be added. We must learn to put him first.

I realize that sounds challenging. When we're bombarded with work obligations, family, social engagements, school, and all the other things that fill up our days, the idea of adding something else can be overwhelming. Understand, though, I'm not talking about putting God on top of everything else. I'm talking about making him the *foundation* on which all the other things rest.

follow the leader

A couple of fishermen named Peter and Andrew were going about their daily tasks, throwing out nets to bring in fish. As we're told in Matthew 4:18–20, Jesus appeared to them and said, "Come."

The amazing thing is, they left their nets "at once" to do what Jesus said. That meant leaving everything they knew and taking a risk. They obviously knew the real deal when they saw it. They recognized Jesus for who he was—the Son of God in their midst—and made a choice to make his will be their new foundation.

A few verses later, the same thing happened with James and John. Once Jesus invited them, they "immediately" dropped everything to follow him. The brothers even left their father, who was in the boat with them, to do so.

> ## Life is the sum of all your choices.
> **—Albert Camus**

When we hear the invitation from Jesus to "come," it's as much about the little things as it is the big stuff. I've heard stories about people who are afraid that if they genuinely surrender to God, they'll have to sell everything they own and move to Africa. That's not necessarily what I'm talking about. For Peter, Andrew, James, and John, the first step was simply to take the first step, not knowing what kind of adventures awaited them.

a little consideration

Maybe there's a first step Jesus is inviting you to take in your own life. Have you ever felt a pull to have some quiet time with God, but you rationalized it away, telling yourself you were too busy? Have you ever thought about giving money to a certain project that the church was involved in, but talked yourself out of it because you had other plans for the cash? Have you ever considered opening up your Bible to read a chapter or two, but turned on the TV or picked up another book instead? What about the other little stuff: simply being nice to other people, being polite in traffic, or being encouraging to your family?

God wants to bless us and give us lives of promise and adventure just as he did with Peter, Andrew, James, and John. But first, he has to know we're serious. We show him our commitment by carrying out the little things, not because we feel like we have to, but because we want to. As it says in Luke 16:10, "Unless you are faithful in small matters, you won't be faithful in large ones."

Now, if you're in any kind of business, you know how this works. If you don't take care of the little stuff, the business can ultimately end up in big trouble. It happens in sports, too.

Dizzy Dean was a pitcher with the St. Louis Cardinals, and he could throw harder than anyone in the major leagues at the time. In 1937, while playing an All-Star game, he hit a ball to the fence. As he was running around the bases and trying to watch the ball, he stubbed his toe on one of the bases and fell.

When he went back to the pitcher's mound, Dean's toe continued to bother him, so he had to adjust for it. Dean changed his pitching style to accommodate the pain in his toe and, suddenly, his famous blue darter pitch was less powerful. He later said his career was cut short because that stubbed toe changed his delivery. Like Dizzy Dean, it's those little things we've got to watch.

focus

In order to make a true commitment, we must also be willing to sacrifice something. Often that means choosing to please God rather than choosing to please other people. If you can get this right, it'll actually save you a lot of trouble, since you can never please everybody all the time anyway.

One day, a man, his son, and their donkey were walking along the road. A group of people saw them and said, "Have you ever seen such a thing? Why do they trudge along the road when they could ride?" Hearing this, the man put the boy on the donkey's back and they continued on.

Another group of people they encountered couldn't believe that the boy would have the nerve to ride while the old man was walking. The man then got up on the donkey and asked the boy to walk alongside.

Still another group called the man lazy and wondered why he didn't let his son ride. Still trying to please everyone, the man put his son on the donkey next to him.

Both of them were riding the donkey when yet another passerby questioned how much they cared for the animal, loading him down in such a manner. He said, "You two fellows are better able to carry the beast than he is to carry you." So they gave that a try, too. The man and his son got down off the donkey, rigged him up to a pole, and carried him over their shoulders.

Unfortunately, while crossing a river, the donkey got spooked and fell into the water. In his efforts to please everyone, the man

> **Every happening, great and small, is a parable whereby God speaks to us, and the art of life is to get the message.**
>
> **—Malcolm Muggeridge**

pleased no one and, on top of everything else, he lost his donkey!

When we try to please everyone, we can lose our own sense of what's right and what's not. In trying to agree with what other people say is important, we lose the ability to think for ourselves.

be deliberate

Commitment involves making a choice about what we're going to believe and who we're going to serve. It means carefully thinking it all through and counting the cost of our decision, in order to make it fully and completely.

It's often said that no one can serve two masters. That's a biblical truth, located in Matthew 6:24: "For you will hate one and love the other, or be devoted to one and despise the other."

As we live in this world today, we must ask ourselves, *Whom do I serve? Who is master in my life?* We can quickly answer when we take a look at where we spend most of our time and energy.

Often, it's not an easy decision because we may feel as if we are in the middle of a balancing act between other people's expectations of us, our expectations of ourselves, and what we believe God expects of us.

But an awesome thing happens when we learn to put God first. He helps us balance out all the rest. When we spend time with him and get to know his ways, we can more clearly distinguish between things that are truly important and lasting, and things that are not. We become accustomed to God's reality, and it more easily becomes our own.

> **God is love. Not cheap, sentimental love, but redeeming love which cannot be said, but must be seen in the way we live.**
>
> **—Harry Denman**

Everything will not be easy once you decide to fully commit to God. That's not the way it works. We're promised in Psalm 34:17 that the Lord will deliver us from our troubles, pretty much a guarantee that we'll have them. Just remember: When the ground we stand on is one of faith and commitment to God, we can be assured that he has a plan for a lives, a solution for our problems, and a hope for our future.

dive in

- *On a scale of one to ten, how committed am I to seeing God as the master of my life?*
- *What things compete with God to take control in my life?*
- *How could making God my top priority change my circumstances?*

chapter 4
finding a niche

Have you ever thought about what it takes to make a person run?

I don't mean what it takes psychologically, what makes a person actually want to pound the pavement for mile after mile after mile, enduring pain, fatigue, and all the other stuff that might come with it.

I mean what it physically takes to make someone run. At first glance, it seems like it's all about the legs. They're propelling the body, after all, getting it where it wants to go. Strong legs are a real asset to a runner; they make a lot of difference when it comes to speed and endurance.

There are also the feet. It's been said that during one hour of strenuous exercise, feet cushion up to a million pounds of pressure. Running, in particular, puts the force of up to five times the body weight onto the foot with every step.

As important as the feet and legs are, though, they're only part of the picture. The knees, for example, have to bend to lift the feet off the ground. The hips help move the legs, and the spine helps hold the body upright. The lungs help the body breathe, the heart pumps blood, and the eyes keep lookout for anything that might be ahead. And that's just for starters.

When you decide to go from a walk to a run, the brain sends signals to pretty much the entire body, because that's what will be needed to make the switch. Every single part of the body is important.

I'm sure that somewhere along the way, you've heard the church referred to as "the Body of Christ." The next time you hear that saying, think about running. Remember that, if the knees had decided to stay in bed, the feet figured they had better things to do, or the lungs were scared that they just didn't know enough to get in the game—then nobody would get anywhere. It's exactly the same in the Body of Christ. It takes every single one of us to make this thing go.

I can't tell you whether you're a foot, a leg, or a knee in the Body of Christ. Some people might be hearts, mouths, or ears, perhaps even elbows, spleens, or toes. The point is, they're all important. No matter where you are in the body, you are the only one of you that God made, and you have a special role that only you can play. He created *you* to help accomplish his work on the earth.

everybody's a winner

Think back to that runner for a minute, and imagine that he's just finished a marathon in first place. The crowds go wild, and a rush of people approach to congratulate him. At that moment, do you think they just honor his legs, his knees, or his elbows? No. When the entire body works together, every part shares in the victory.

It is the same thing for us as Christians. If we take part in praying for something to happen, we share in the joy when it does. If we help to financially support a missionary, we share in the rewards when people come to believe. When we take the time to reach out to a neighbor who's sick by making a meal, or volunteer to teach a child in Sunday school, we benefit when those people's lives change.

> ## It's not who you are that holds you back, it's who you think you're not.
> **—Author Unknown**

You never know how many lives you might be touching. Samuel Wesley, for instance, was a pastor many years ago in England. He and his wife had nineteen children. (And, no, I can't imagine that, either.) At that time, England was at its worst morally, ethically, and biblically, so Wesley joined a lot of people in asking God to send revival there.

The problem was, since Wesley had so many children, he had no private place to pray. His prayers were constantly interrupted by his young children, two of whom were named Charles and John. Little did Wesley know that the answer to his prayers for revival was right there at his feet.

John would later become known as the father of Methodism, and Charles would go on to write more than nine thousand hymns and poems. The impact of their lives—not only on the country of England but also on the world and the kingdom—was immensely powerful.

Their father played his part. Wesley was present in the moment and willing to step up to the plate. When we do that, an incredible thing happens: God sets us up to win. God doesn't play by the same rules the world does. The world tells us that certain things will give us purpose, that it's all about us; but it's really not. It's about being part of the Body of Christ, part of the bigger picture—and fully realizing our importance in it.

made by design

God's Word, the Bible, teaches that you were beautifully and perfectly designed by God just as you are. You're not an accident, and you didn't just happen. As David said in Psalm 139:15–16:

> You watched me as I was being formed in utter seclusion,
>   as I was woven together in the dark of the womb.
> You saw me before I was born.
> Every day of my life was recorded in your book.
> Every moment was laid out before a single day had passed

And God made you the way you are.

Years ago, there was a beautiful, brown-eyed Irish girl by the name of Amy Carmichael. Some of her friends had blue eyes, and she desperately wanted blue eyes, too. Amy was a committed Christian and knew God answered prayers, so one night, she petitioned God to change the color of her eyes. The next morning, full of faith, she went to look in the mirror. Her eyes were still brown.

God didn't answer "yes" to that prayer, but he did do something else. Later in life, Amy Carmichael became a missionary to India and rescued children from prostitution in Hindu temples. She would stain her skin and dress in saris to pass as Hindu to help the children. Blue eyes would have given her away.

If we decide to live our lives according to what we want, we run the very real risk of missing God's purpose. If we choose to live according to what God wants for us, we're on the way to having a rich, fulfilling, and rewarding life.

It's been said that there are three different kinds of people in every institution: risk-takers, caretakers, and undertakers. Risk-takers are willing to start things. The caretakers just want to hang on to the way things are, and the undertakers want to bury them. Unfortunately, in the last century, more churches have been buried than are in existence today. Perhaps that's because there aren't enough risk-takers. Are we willing to hear God's call, believe in what he says, and take a risk?

all things are possible

Let's talk about the Olympics. Since the very first Olympic games in Greece, the goal had been to break the four-minute mile. For hundreds of years, however, nobody could run a mile in less than four minutes, so they decided it was impossible.

Along came twenty-five-year-old Roger Bannister, who in 1954 became the first person to break that record, finishing the mile in three minutes and 59.4 seconds. Here's an interesting fact: More than thirty other people also ran a mile in under four minutes that very same year. The year after that, hundreds more did—all because they saw it could be done.

God's gifts put man's best dreams to shame.
—Elizabeth Barrett Browning

The world will tell us that things are impossible. People will tell us that we're not significant, or that we're not fit for the tasks to which we're called. They might even try to tell us that working on a relationship with God is impossible or isn't worth the effort.

I disagree. The Bible tells us that, with man, some things are indeed impossible. But according to Matthew 19:27, "with God everything is possible."

Bannister had to believe that the impossible was possible, or he never would have tried to run the race. He must have believed that he could make a difference and have a lasting impact on the world around him.

group effort

There's something else you need to know about that race: Bannister wasn't running the race alone. He most likely couldn't have succeeded alone, either. It's not often mentioned, but it was a carefully planned race, and a couple of pacesetters ran it along with Bannister. One ran in front of him and the other behind, so Bannister could stay at the pace he needed to be at to break the record. In the middle of the race, the one behind ran ahead, and the one who had been leading fell back behind Bannister. That way, neither of the pacesetters was too taxed. In the last stretch, Bannister picked up speed, lengthened his stride, and finished the race alone.

At that particular moment, with the encouragement of others around him and the faith that it could be done, Bannister fulfilled one of God's purposes for his life. It wasn't long after that, though, that he retired from competitive running. Bannister was a medical student at the time of that "miracle" mile. He completed his studies and became a consultant neurologist.

Your calling may not be to break a world record or to be a doctor. One thing is certain, however: You were created with intent and for specific reasons. Your willingness to take your place on the track will put you a step closer to discovering—and fulfilling—God's intentions.

We have a chance, individually and corporately, to both run the race *and* to win it. This is a much larger race than just the one we see here on earth. We have the opportunity, like Wesley, Bannister, and others, to impact the future long after we've breathed our last breath here on earth.

dive in

- *Am I a functioning part of the Body of Christ? Why or why not?*
- *Has there ever been a time I should have stepped up to the plate, but didn't? What was the result?*
- *How could God use me if I were committed to following his lead, instead of my own?*

God has not called us to see through each other,
but to see each other through.

—*Author Unknown*

chapter 5
love your neighbor

There's a song called "They'll Know We Are Christians," and it has a great chorus. It says, "And they'll know we are Christians by our love, by our love. Yes, they'll know we are Christians by our love."

What comes to mind when you hear the word "Christian"? What sets a Christian apart from everyone else? I hope it's in the way he or she lives life. At its best, the Christian life is one of joy, faith, peace, and—of course—love.

But what does "love" really mean? Take a look at what Jesus said in the Bible verse on which the hymn is based, John 13:34–35:

So now I am giving you a new commandment: Love each other. Just as I have loved you, you should love each other. Your love for one another will prove to the world that you are my disciples.

Understand the kind of love that Jesus is talking about isn't the kind of thing you'll find in songs and movies today. He's not talking about some kind of swept away, emotional feeling. He is talking about a conscious choice. That's the kind of love that's described in 1 Corinthians 13:4–8:

> Love is patient and kind. Love is not jealous or boastful or proud or rude. Love does not demand its own way. Love is not irritable, and it keeps no record of when it has been wronged. It is never glad about injustice but rejoices whenever the truth wins out. Love never gives up, never loses faith, is always hopeful, and endures through every circumstance.

But let's be honest. Do most of us love the other members of God's family like that? What about within our churches, within our church family? Do we love each other so above and beyond the world's definition of love that the world actually sits up and takes notice?

We could.

The key to that is found in John 13. Jesus said, "Just as I have loved you." Yes, God expects us to be committed to fully loving others, and he also provides the way for us to do it— through the love of Jesus. His love for us provides an extravagant example for us to imitate.

love in action

A group of businessmen once visited a leprosarium while they were in Korea. A beautiful American nurse was tending the patients, and one of the men commented to another that, if she was in America, she could be making a good living, rather than having to work there with those who had leprosy. Another man in the group commented directly to the nurse that he wouldn't do what she did for a million dollars.

"Neither would I," she replied. But for the love of Jesus Christ, she did.

Once we allow the love of Jesus to really penetrate the walls of our hearts, we get so full of that love that we can't help but overflow. We learn how to see other people the way Jesus sees them: doing the best they can with what they've got to work with. Through the eyes of Jesus, we are able to look at the people around us, not as who they actually are, but as who they could be. We then begin to do things, even little things, that can help them reach their potential.

A man named Bill Lemley said a great thing: "When nobody around you seems to measure up, it's time to check your yardstick." Let's check our yardsticks against the yardsticks of Christ.

In 1 Thessalonians 5:11, we're told to "encourage each other and build each other up, just as you are already doing." It's so easy to tear each other down, isn't it? But if we truly love each other—if we allow God to love others through us—then we'll focus on helping others succeed. We'll be willing to get our eyes off of ourselves for a while and put them on someone else.

> ## People see God every day.
> ## They just don't recognize him.
> **—Pearl Bailey**

I once visited a home where a huge mirror had been placed in the middle of the front door. I saw my reflection, and I remember thinking to myself that it was an odd place for a mirror. I tried to imagine why the homeowners would choose to have such a thing on their door. When I entered the foyer, I turned around to look back at the mirror and comment on it. It was then that I realized it was actually a window, not a mirror. This allowed the homeowners to look from the inside to see who is at their door without being observed from the outside. Visitors merely see their own images.

I thought about that for a while. And I realized that every single one of us is either looking at life like a mirror (seeing only ourselves and what's in it for us), or like a window (through which God allows us to focus on those around us).

acceptance and forgiveness

Another part of really loving those around us is to accept them, just as Christ accepted us. If we do this, according to Romans 15:7, "then God will be glorified." This means loving even though they might be hard to love, and accepting that God made them uniquely who they are. They might be different from us, but who's to say who's wrong and who's right? In 1 Corinthians 13, we're told that love is not irritable. In other words, it means we're willing to let go of all those little things that other people do that nag at us. We're willing to admit that, in the grand scheme of things, those things really aren't that important.

That goes hand in hand with Colossians 3:13, which urges us to "make allowance for each other's faults and forgive the person who offends you." Forgiveness, like love, is a choice. For example, God chooses to forgive us of all the wrongs we've done, if we're willing to let him. Jesus was also willing to forgive even those who abused him, mocked him, and hung him on a cross to die. It's recorded in Luke 23:34 that while on that cross, Jesus prayed, "Father, forgive these people, because they don't know what they are doing." Not only had Jesus forgiven them himself, he even went so far as to plead for their mercy with God.

That's all part of the idea that love "keeps no record of when it has been wronged." It doesn't really matter what someone did yesterday, because we all make mistakes. We have to be careful about the grudges we hold. They don't really hurt the people we're holding the grudges against; they only hurt us. When we hold on to a wrong in our past, it's the same as telling God that we won't allow him to work in the situation. It's the same as telling him that the wrong was, in our eyes, bigger than he and his ability to handle it.

Do you know what happens when we think something is bigger than God? It becomes an idol in our lives, and it eventually causes separation between us and God. So please, if there's someone who has hurt you, ask God to help you forgive so you can move on to where you're supposed to be. Society tells us that we should maintain that what's-in-it-for-me mentality; but Christ reminds us to ask what could be in it for other people.

> **If reconciliation is God's chief business, it is ours.**
>
> **—E. Stanley Jones**

When we're told that love "is always hopeful," I tend to think it always hopes for the best in everyone. It may be that the person who hurt you never intended to at all. It's important to realize that, if you're willing to forgive others, sooner or later you'll find that others are more likely to forgive you, too. And once a family—especially a church family—becomes quick to forgive, that's the kind of family that other people want to be a part of. They'll see it as a place that they can be accepted, faults and all.

humility and authenticity

People also want to be a part of a church family that's living in harmony, as we're urged to do in Romans 12:16. "Don't try to act important, but enjoy the company of ordinary people. And don't think you know it all!" How sad it is when we come across as thinking we're better than others, or that we have all the answers! Sooner or later, as it's long been said, "Pride comes before a fall." Sooner or later, the one doing the judging is the one who will be judged.

In John 13:1–17, there's a beautiful story about Jesus and his closest followers, the disciples. It takes place during his last days on earth, and he chooses to spend his time teaching a valuable lesson about humble service to others. Rather than focusing on himself, he chooses to wash their feet. No doubt those feet were stinky, sweaty, and dirty. Yet, they became his priority. He focuses on the job that nobody else would want to take on, and in doing so, offers a true picture of selflessness. It's an attitude that can make all of us think twice about what we believe we're above doing.

Look at Romans 12:10, and you'll find that we're expected to "love each other with genuine affection and take delight in honoring each other." How often do we really see that happening?

If I only had a little humility, I would be perfect.

—Ted Turner

Many people attend church because they think they can get something out of it. Some attend because it will keep peace with someone else in their family who really wants them to go. Some think they're doing something they should do. Some even attend because being part of a certain congregation is good for their social standing or public image. Sadly, they're missing the whole point.

The church was created to help people know God and to walk in relationship with him. Everyone there is created in God's own image, thus, it is only by experiencing others that we can experience all of him. Truly experiencing others means learning to love them. It means choosing to love them, and allowing them to love us in return.

It isn't always easy to be part of a church family, but I can tell you it's worth it. When we're willing to open our eyes to the beauty in others, all sorts of wonderful things happen. We begin to understand what love truly is, and just how very much God loves us. Enough to forgive us, to hold no record of our wrongs, and to protect us. Enough to be patient with us and to be kind. A great example to follow, indeed.

dive in

- *What's my biggest challenge when it comes to loving other people?*
- *How could God change that?*
- *Is there anyone that I'm holding a grudge against? If so, what can I do to turn the situation around?*

When we are no longer able to change a situation,
we are challenged to change ourselves.

—*Viktor Frankl*

chapter 6

overcoming obstacles

O ne of America's favorite pastimes—and I'll never understand it—is to make New Year's resolutions. We pledge to exercise, to take more vacations, or to lose weight. Those resolutions typically don't last past January or, if we're really serious, February.

It seems as if there's always something working against us, doesn't it? Well, there is—the devil. According to Scripture, his main job is to "steal and kill and destroy" (John 10:10). One way he goes about this is to tempt us.

Understand, first of all, that there is no truth in the old saying, "The devil made me do it." The fact is, the devil has no power to make you or me do anything. You and I make choices, and we make them every day of our lives.

temptation

I heard about a man who asked his coworkers to pray for him. This man had made a resolution to quit eating crème-filled doughnuts, so his coworkers agreed to pray that he wouldn't yield to the temptation. They prayed for him for several weeks.

One day, he walked in with a big chocolate-covered crème doughnut in his hand. Someone asked him what had happened to his resolution.

He said, "Oh, this? It's no problem. God said it's OK. This morning I prayed, 'Lord, if you don't want me to have a crème-filled doughnut, then don't let me find a parking place in front of the bakery.' And the tenth time around the block this morning, there was a parking place right there in front of the bakery."

Obviously, this is a bit of an exaggeration. But how many of us have been there, putting ourselves right in the middle of a tempting situation—and then wondering why we caved in?

You may even have experienced something similar since you've started this study. As we've talked about our thirst for more, you may have been—I *hope* you have been—inspired to step out a little more, take a risk or two. If you haven't yet, I believe you will be inspired to seek more as you continue this study.

As this happens, pay attention. Make no mistake, there will be roadblocks and challenges to living the glorious life you're called to live. I can guarantee that the devil, your enemy, would much rather keep you exactly where you are. Only with God's help can you overcome every single challenge.

If you're going through hell, keep going.

—Winston Churchill

Maybe you've committed to read your Bible or pray every day. It's almost a sure bet that the devil will try to distract you with other things. They'll probably look really good to you, too, because Satan is an intelligent adversary. He pays attention to what made us slip up last time, and will try the same trick again and again for as long as he gets away with it.

It's important to remember, though, that's it's not a sin to be tempted. Jesus himself was tempted. It's what we do with temptation that makes all the difference; it's when we yield to it that it becomes sin.

understanding sin

There's that word—*sin*. It's a word that most people outside the church—and perhaps many inside the church—don't really understand. From the outside looking in, sin looks like a list of fun things we can't do without getting in trouble with God. The Christian life, sad to say, can be misrepresented as a dry list of rules and regulations that we have to follow if we want any hope of getting into heaven.

That's not the case at all. When God asks us not to do something—whether it be not committing murder or not gossiping about someone else—he asks us for our own benefit. He sees not only where we've been and where we are now, but also where we're going. He knows what the long-term effects of our sinful behaviors can be.

Understanding the idea of sin doesn't come from just looking at God's side of the equation, however. We also have to look at our own. As we grow deeper in our relationship with God, we come to see that our sins actually hurt God, just as it hurts us when we ask our children not to do something and they do it anyway. Once we're in true relationship with God, deciding whether or not to give in to temptation becomes an easier choice. We decide to do the right thing more often because we want to please the One we love—the One who also loves us more than we can imagine.

Something else happens, too. The more we resist temptation, the stronger we get. The more we see God help us out, the more we realize we can depend on him, as well.

God promised in 1 Corinthians 10:13 that he will not allow you to be tempted more than you can bear. When you are tempted, "he will show you a way out so that you will not give in to it."

If asked to define the word *temptation*, you would probably say something like, "to entice or persuade somebody to do wrong," just like we've been talking about above. However, when the word is used in Matthew 4, in which Jesus is tempted directly by Satan, it translates from the original language as "to test or to prove." Temptation, then, becomes a test. And if we pass it, we become stronger. If we fail that test, though, it can ultimately lead to death.

Call on God, but row away from the rocks.

—Indian proverb

As you read this, you may not think you have any trouble with temptation. But if that's the case, I'd caution you to give it some thought. If you don't think you're tempted by anything, maybe Satan has you so much that he doesn't even need to tempt you any more. The Bible teaches us in James 1:14–15 that, as we grow in faith, every single one of us will be tempted and tested.

Yet temptation isn't all bad . . . it can propel us into good. In James 1:2–4, we read:

Whenever trouble comes your way let it be an opportunity for joy. For when your faith is tested, your endurance has a chance to grow. So let it grow, for when your endurance is fully developed, you will be strong in character and ready for anything.

Consider that we are all tempted by different things. One person, for example, may struggle with alcohol. Another may be tempted to lie. Someone else might be wooed by constant shopping trips, and someone else might be tempted by money.

three temptations

When Satan tempted Jesus, the temptations came in three categories—the same ones that still apply to us. First, in Matthew 4:2–3, he tempted Jesus in the area of physical appetite. At that point, Jesus had been in the wilderness for forty days with nothing to eat. So Satan taunted him: "If you are the Son of God, change these stones into loaves of bread." Of course, Jesus could have done it in an instant. If he had, though, he would have yielded to the temptation that Satan put before him, the desire to satisfy his physical appetite. Jesus knew that, before long, he'd just be hungry again.

Wouldn't it be great if we had that kind of willpower, knowing that what we're tempted by won't really satisfy for long? Be it sexual temptation, the desire for more material things, or the pursuit of other kinds of gratification, we'll ultimately find that kind of appetite is never satisfied.

Satan also tempted Jesus with the idea of exception. In Matthew 4:6, Satan had carried Jesus up to the highest point of the Temple and dared him to jump off. It was a long way down, but he tells Jesus that God would command his angels to lift Jesus up so he wouldn't be harmed. The implication was that the fall would kill anyone else, but Jesus was so special he was an exception.

Have you ever been tempted that way? Ever think something can happen to other people, but surely not to you? For example, dallying in drugs, believing there's no way you could ever get addicted, or thinking you'll never get a speeding ticket because you drive a certain type of vehicle. That's foolishness. We've got to stay on our guard.

We've also got to be wary of the third temptation: power. Satan tried that one on Jesus, too. In Matthew 4:8–9, Satan had taken Jesus to the top of a mountain and offered him a kingdom as far as the eye could see.

Don't we find that tempting? Don't we want power and prestige? We all want to be popular, and some are willing to sell their souls to get it. But not Jesus; he held firm and resisted. We can, too, with God's help.

scriptural strategy
Here's the key: The next time you find yourself tempted—whether it's to satisfy your physical appetite, be an exception to the rule, or to become more powerful—remember what Jesus did. He stood on the Word of God, and he told the devil to leave him alone.

> Some Christians have a very small Savior,
> for they are not willing to
> receive him fully, and let him do
> great and mighty things for them.
> —Dwight L. Moody

When Satan tried to get him to turn the stones into bread, Jesus said, "The Scriptures say, 'People need more than bread for their life; they must feed on every word of God.'" When Satan tried to get him to jump, Jesus replied, "The Scriptures also say, 'Do not test the Lord your God.'" And finally, when Satan tried to get him to take the kingdom in exchange for his devotion, Jesus said, "Get out of here, Satan. For the Scriptures say, 'You must worship the Lord your God; serve only him.'"

Do you know what happened next? Satan, defeated, left him alone. Jesus acted aggressively when he commanded Satan to leave, and we should do the same. The longer any of us lingers in a tempting situation, the more likely it is that we'll yield to it. The quicker we get out, the more likely we are to successfully resist.

Remember, you'll no doubt face temptations and distractions in coming days. When you do, stay the course, and keep James 4:7 in mind. It says, "Resist the devil, and he will flee from you." This is because God's in charge of the world, not Satan. He has no authority here, other than the authority you give him. And if you let Satan hang around long enough, he'll take whatever authority he can get.

dive in

- *How could the enemy try to keep me from moving ahead in my walk with God?*
- *How could God help me fight temptation?*
- *Who in my life could I confide in and ask for prayer in overcoming temptation?*

How wonderful it is that nobody need wait a single moment
before starting to improve the world.

—Anne Frank

chapter 7

time to commit

The wedding vows of a celebrity couple say a lot about our current society. Instead of the old-fashioned pledges of "'til death do us part," this couple promised to take care of one another "as long as our love survives." Now, really, how long do you think that will be?

In a world with increasingly popular phrases like "exit strategy" and "keeping my options open," these vows fit the mold. No matter how we put it, we're all saying the same thing—we're not fully committed.

Commitment is the starting point of virtually any relationship. Marriage begins with a vow; a new job begins with an agreement detailing responsibilities and compensation; and even joining the church involves commitment to God and fellow believers.

Commitment is the foundation on which everything else will be built. Commitment is like that glass of water in the restaurant; it's not flashy, and many times, something else will look tastier. Even if other things look good, they won't satisfy us in the same way that knowing where we belong, knowing who is there for us, and resting securely in God's love will. All these things are available for the taking.

We'll review some major points and dig a little deeper before moving on.

recognizing the need

By now, of course, you know there is more. With any luck, you've become aware of the areas in which you were thirsty and didn't even know it, places where you felt empty but couldn't say why. There's a joy in that revelation, a peace in discovering the emptiness even if it's not yet filled. Continuing this study will go a long way toward helping to water those thirsty parts of your heart.

But don't expect to get to the end and be totally satisfied. The whole point is to show you how to continually satisfy that thirst. While Jesus promised the Samaritan woman that he had water that would allow her not to thirst again, there is something beautiful in the pursuit of God, a realization that we can never quite get enough.

For what am I thirsty?

our wellspring

God will do anything to draw us to him, even if it means going out of his way to reach us as he did with the Samaritan woman. God pursues us with intention. I love what it says about Jesus: he *had* to go to Samaria. He had to go for one reason: to encounter that woman at the well.

But God's commitment to us doesn't end when we come to him. Nor is it merely delayed until we get to heaven. God promises in Isaiah 55:3, "I am ready to make an everlasting covenant with you. I will give you all the mercies and unfailing love that I promised to David."

God wants to be involved in the major and minor details of our lives. How often do we put off prayer until we have a major decision to make? How many times do we wait until we're in a crisis to ask for help? It doesn't have to only be that way. God wants to be here for us every day. Have you ever considered that God might put on dazzling displays just to get our attention? He creates a stunning sunrise, a captivating sunset, and a breathtaking moon. How often, though, do we get lost in the busyness of our day and miss God altogether? God desperately wants to share each day with us, no matter how ordinary it is.

Think about the last time you went strolling down memory lane with a dear friend or relative. What memories did you recall? Chances are, it wasn't that vacation-of-a-lifetime and it probably wasn't Christmas or some other holiday. No, most likely what caused the most laughs and memories was something that, on its face, wasn't that big of a deal. It was just an ordinary day when an extraordinary moment happened.

God wants to make those kinds of memories with us, too. Yes, God is big enough to handle the big problems that come our way. God also wants to be there when we land that big promotion or buy our first house. Remember, though, God wants to be involved in the little things, too. He wants us to take joy in the sunsets and to bring him the stubbed toes of life. God does care—about both the big and the small.

What do I need to take to God that I thought was too small for him?

great expectations

You were created to be in relationship with God. Outside of that relationship, you'll always feel an emptiness. You'll always feel you don't quite measure up, even if you can't put a finger on it. Basically, God wants from you what he's offered you: an everlasting covenant. He wants you to also be committed to that relationship. Granted, there's mercy when you fail and grace when you turn away from that relationship temporarily; but God is always there, calling you back.

The parable of the lost sheep in Luke 15:1–7 tells of the shepherd who went looking for the one lost sheep, though he left ninety-nine behind to do so. God is just like that shepherd; he wants all of his sheep, including the one who may have wandered away.

Being committed to our relationship with God presents itself in many forms. There's prayer, of course, when we really have conversations with God. There's presence in a church family, where we partner with others to accomplish what he wants from us. There are gifts, where we share freely with God what he's given us. And there's service, where we help carry our weight in the Body of Christ. (We'll talk about those commitments in the coming weeks.) These four treasures are an outgrowth of a healthy relationship with God, not four tasks that we can check off as a substitute for that relationship.

What will it take for me to give God more of myself?

finding a niche

God doesn't just call us into a relationship with him; he also wants us to be in relationship with other Christians. We can accomplish so much more together than we can on our own. So often, though, we look for the place where we fit. We pick out a church based on how close it is to our home, whether we know people there, or whether we like the style of music.

There may be fifty things we'd prefer in a church. Maybe we like our sermons with a bit of humor or a ton of Scriptures. Maybe we like rock, not Bach. The list could go on and on. But choosing a church isn't like choosing a restaurant, determined by how well you like what's being offered. Sometimes God will put us into a family of believers precisely because we don't fit.

You may be the only gray-haired person in a church of all younger people. Perhaps they need your wisdom. You may be the only single person in a body of married couples. Maybe they need to know how to minister to people who aren't like them.

It could be that you're a new mom in a body where most of the mothers are raising teenagers. Those mothers might be honored to be asked to share their advice and to be needed.

Joining a particular church body is answering a call. God has a specific place where he wants to place you, and it may not always be comfortable.

As with any other commitment, though, we're supposed to follow through. That means staying there as long as God keeps us there. It doesn't mean we stay as long as we like the music or until the pastor says something that stomps on our toes. It doesn't mean we leave at the first sign of a perceived slight or the first Sunday the sermon stretches on a little too long.

Sometimes the best lessons we can learn are from those who are most unlike us.

Am I in a church in which I'm called or merely comfortable?

love defined

Let's be clear on this. You will not like every person you meet, at least not initially. You won't even like every person in your church. There are people you're going to clash with. There are people with different political views, as well as people whose place in life is so vastly different from yours that you have little in common.

God never commanded us to *like* everyone, though. He commands us to love our neighbors as we love ourselves. (Note— it says *as*, not *more than*, not *less than*.) Love is a conscious choice. Like is an emotion. Love is so much more powerful than like, of course, especially when it comes from the conscious act.

As we make this conscious choice, we allow Jesus to love other people through us. We might even start to see them as God sees them. We might begin to understand that they've been hurt, or that they've suffered great setbacks. We may see the good qualities they possess, even if those qualities come in a package that rubs us the wrong way. This doesn't mean that we have to invite them over for dinner on a regular basis. It just means that we treat them with decency, kindness, and love. Of course, as we make the conscious choice to love our church family, we may just find that we grow to like them, too.

Who do I need to love, regardless of how I feel about them?

overcoming obstacles

We know *who* wants to stand in our way. It can be pretty easy, however, to blame the devil when he's not always the one at fault. Remember that, just as Jesus overcame the devil's temptations, God promises us that we also will be able to do this. So, if it's the devil who is preventing you from committing fully to God and to others, resist him and he will leave you alone. God's Word promises that.

Have you considered the possibility that you may be the one standing in your own way? Could you be allowing a past hurt to prevent you from giving your heart away fully? Could you be unwilling because you don't want to give up that much control? Could it be that you don't believe God wants a relationship with you?

Remember, commitment to God and to our church family is the foundation on which we'll build during the next five weeks. God is calling you into deeper water in the area of commitment.

Am I willing to get a little more wet?

part II
drawing
water

chapter 8

tapping into the source

Ever been to the desert?

It's dry, and it's hot. The sun relentlessly beats down on you, and every step you take kicks up a little more dust. There might be a little wind, but all it does is lift up that dust and spin it around. The dust doesn't really go anywhere, it just clings to you. Then you're covered in the stuff, and you start to wonder if you'll ever be clean again.

Now, it's easy enough to imagine a desert such as those located in the American West. Have you ever felt, though, like you're in a desert in your everyday life? Every step drains you. No matter where you look, there's no new life. Dust and other junk are all around you, and dirt covers you from head to toe. You have this sense of wandering aimlessly, barely existing, with nothing but reminders of what might have been, could have been, if only there had been a little water. Any of this sound familiar?

Water makes the difference between life and death. In fact, in the history of civilization, people always looked first for a water supply to determine the locale of a settlement. One way people found a water supply was by looking at the vegetation. Water is essential to every living thing. So the places where you find lush plants and fruitful trees are the places where that water has been, and where that water continues to flow.

When we lose God, it is not God who is lost.
—Author Unknown

So let me ask you something. Is there any part of your life that's arid and desert-like at the moment? Where's the water? When was the last time you actively sought the oasis of God's presence? When was the last time you watered your spirit through prayer?

We all go through times when it seems like God is distant or that our prayers aren't being heard. It's all part of the ebb and flow of him drawing us closer, teaching us to pursue him with our whole being and to wait for him.

Sometimes, though, we can reach a place in which we literally feel all alone. Our spirit feels so dry that we can almost taste dust in our throat. At times like that, we might even feel forgotten, and the temptation is to just give up trying to break through to the next level.

In Isaiah 44:3, however, the prophet delivered a promise from God to the people of Israel that applies as much to us as it did to them. God said, "For I will give you abundant water to quench your thirst and to moisten your parched fields. And I will pour out my Spirit and my blessings on your children."

planted in grace

We're going to dive into the topic of prayer now. We'll look at what it is, what it's not, how to do it, why to do it, and what happens when you do it. There's an image I want you to keep in mind as we take a look at prayer. I want you to imagine a tree—a strong, tall tree with full branches and overflowing fruit. A tree planted right by the riverside, with constant access to living water.

If you're not sure what a tree has to do with your prayer life, simply refer to the very first Psalm. David said that there are two kinds of people in this life: the blessed and the wicked. The ones who are blessed, the ones who delight in the Lord, "are like trees planted along the riverbank, bearing fruit each season without fail. Their leaves never wither, and in all they do, they prosper."

Notice that he called the trees "planted." When you come to the point that you submit your life to Jesus Christ, that life becomes planted in grace. And if you try to plant yourself some other way, any other way than through God's grace, that planting won't be firm.

Jesus told a parable about this in Matthew 13:1–9. One day, a man went out and scattered seed, which landed on all sorts of different soil. Some of the seed fell on hard ground and could not even penetrate the dirt. It did nothing but die. Some of the seed went into the ground, landing just under the topsoil. It began to sprout, but it scorched and died as soon as the sun came out because it had no root system. Some of the seed, however, fell on good soil. It went down into the ground, formed a root system, and began to grow and produce fruit.

When we, as Christians, become trees that are firmly planted, it means that we go down into that good, fertile, well-watered soil, and form a root system. We're told by Jesus in John 15:5, "I am the vine; you are the branches. Those who remain in me, and I in them, will produce much fruit."

root system

The way we connect to God and soak up that living water is through prayer. What he expects of our lives is that we're willing to be lined up with what he wants us to be. He'll provide the streams of waters in direction, encouragement, discipline, and love. Then, if we're willing to be firmly planted, we'll grow.

One of the tallest trees in America is the sequoia. A particular tall one is called the General Sherman, and it's 272 feet high. It's been estimated that forty five-room houses could be built with the wood from that one tree.

Contrast that with another tree, the bonsai. The Japanese-developed tree has tap roots that are clipped so they can't grow. The trees only grow to be about eighteen inches high, becoming something of a novelty or a decorative piece. People might look at a bonsai and say, "Isn't it pretty? Doesn't it look good?" But, it can never grow, because it has no root system.

An interesting fact is that the seeds of the giant sequoia and the bonsai are the same size. How they grow all depends on how they're planted. One, with no root system, probably won't reach two feet tall; the other, when planted by a stream of water, can reach almost three hundred feet.

What about you? Are you like that bonsai? Or are you like the sequoia? How much are you willing to allow God's grace to come into your life and to be planted by the streams of water? Remember that God says he's already planted you. It's up to you, however, to reach those roots down deep and catch a drink.

No man can follow Christ and go astray.
—William H. P. Faunce

What will happen when you do? Just like any well-planted, well-watered tree, you'll start to produce.

Remember, the most important thing about a tree is not how pretty it looks or the structure of the limbs; it's about what kind of fruit it produces. I have some friends in Clanton, Alabama, who grow peaches. They tell me you can never measure a peach tree by what the leaves look like. You measure the tree by what the peaches look like. Some of the scrawniest trees can grow the best peaches and some of the ugliest trees can produce the most beautiful peaches.

In Luke 6:43–44, Jesus said: "A good tree can't produce bad fruit, and a bad tree can't produce good fruit. A tree is identified by the kind of fruit it produces." The secret to good fruit is to stay connected to him, the source of life.

In that first Psalm, we're told that the blessed man who is like a tree planted by streams of water and who produces fruit in season—his leaf never withers. In other words, the replenishing, growth, and sustenance that he experiences is permanent. The blessed man's leaves don't wither up like the leaves of the tree in the desert.

permanent fixture

Very few things are permanent in this day and age. We want disposable things. We want diapers that we don't have to wash and dishes we don't have to clean. Are you wearing clothes today that you wore twenty-five years ago, driving the same car you drove twenty-five years ago, or even still living in the same house? Probably not. We spend most of our time and energy on things that are not very permanent.

The blessed person, by contrast, is interested not just in the temporary but also in the eternal. Jesus told us this in John 6:27:

> But you shouldn't be so concerned about perishable things like food. Spend your energy seeking the eternal life that I, the Son of Man, can give you. For God the Father has sent me for that very purpose.

The most permanent thing in life is Jesus Christ. Everything else changes, but he never does. In fact, in Hebrews 13:8, it says: "Jesus Christ is the same yesterday, today, and forever." Connecting with him, then, is to be part of something that matters, something that's eternal and permanent.

A friend of mine has an exceptionally beautiful flower garden. I recently asked him how he got the plants to grow. To my surprise, he answered, "I come out and spank 'em every morning."

I said, "You do what?"

And he replied, "I spank 'em." He said that when you put a plant in the ground, it has a tendency to collect dead dirt around it. He goes out every morning with a newspaper in hand, and then hits his plants. This process disturbs their root systems, which causes the plants to seek new, more alive dirt. The result is that the plants grow more.

Apart from God every activity is merely a passing whiff of insignificance.

—Alfred North Whitehead

As you learn more about prayer, you might find that your root system needs to be disturbed a little bit. Maybe you're like that flower or that withering tree. Maybe you've let the dead dirt pile up to the point that you're not even sure you can move it. Just remember what Ezekiel said, God can change even a desert into a fertile field.

dive in

- *On a scale of one to ten—one being as dry as the desert and ten being lush, well-watered, fruitful, and vibrant— how would I rate my prayer life?*
- *When was the last time I found myself in the desert? What led me there, and how did I find my way out?*
- *How can I make sure God's living water continuously flows into my life?*

Prayer is exhaling the spirit of man and
inhaling the spirit of God.

—*Edwin Keith*

chapter 9
prayer defined

L et's have a conversation.

I don't mean you and me. I mean us and God.

I don't believe God is up in heaven, sitting by some special phone, waiting for us to call. I believe he never hung up from the last time we talked. He's just waiting, once again, for me—or you—to continue our conversation. And the way we do that is through prayer.

This can be a concept that many people find difficult to understand. Many think prayer has to be formal, or that it has to include certain words or rituals. That's not the case, however. Prayer is simply talking to God.

I heard a story about a young man at a downtown city church. Every afternoon at five o'clock, he walked into the church, and every day, forty-five minutes later, he would come out.

Now, people working around the area started to notice. And one day someone asked him: "Why is it that you go into the church building every day at five? What is it you're doing in there?"

And he responded, "I pray."

Well, of course, the person was still curious. So here came the next questions: "You pray? What do you mean? How do you do that?"

And he said, "I walk into the church, and I kneel at the altar, and I just sit there for a moment. And then I say, 'God, this is Joe.' Before long, I hear him say, 'Joe, this is God.' Then I share my heart with him, and he shares his heart with me. And those are the best minutes of my day."

You can have that, too. Prayer is just talking to God. It's sharing your heart with him. It's setting aside a specific time when God invites me into his presence and we have a conversation. Conversations involve both talking and listening, and so should prayer. When we're willing to listen, God will share with us his vision for our lives, his encouragement, and his love.

A well-known saying is, "Prayer changes things." I don't think that's completely accurate. I'm not sure if prayer changes *things*, but I know that prayer changes *people*, and people change things.

be careful what you ask for

Prayer really changed David. In Psalm 139:23–24, he wrote:

Search me, O God, and know my heart;
    test me and know my thoughts.
Point out anything in me that offends you,
    and lead me along the path of everlasting life.

Do we really want to be searched by God? What David was saying was, "I want you to test me. Put me to the test so you can know my thoughts." And when he said, "Point out anything in me that offends you"—boy, that was dangerous. Have you asked your husband or your wife or your best friend to point out anything about you that offends them? I didn't think so. These are the people we trust most . . . yet we don't even share everything with them. God, however, knows everything about us.

Asking God to search you, then, is like going through airport security. The X-ray machine allows the screeners to see everything in your luggage. That's basically what David asked for in this Psalm: "God, I want to put myself in front of you like an X-ray machine. Know my thoughts, my motives, my heart. Point it out to me, God, and I'm going to listen to you. You show me what I need to know."

So there it is. Prayer is both talking and listening.

> Before we can pray, "Lord, thy kingdom come," we must be willing to pray, "My kingdom go."
>
> **—Alan Redpath**

confidentially speaking

While we're at it, let's consider what prayer is *not*. First of all, it's not a religious activity, something you do just for the sake of doing it. Jesus said in Matthew 6:5: "When you pray, don't be like the hypocrites." Prayer, for them, was just a ritual, and they would do it in public so everyone would see them. Granted, sometimes prayer involves rituals, like when we say a blessing before a meal, or when we go to a meeting and they open it with all heads bowed. But really, prayer is not religious at all. At its best, prayer is just like talking to a close friend and, as I mentioned earlier, sharing your heart.

You can share everything with God, things that you can't share with anyone else. Since he knows it all anyway and knows the end from the beginning, it's not like you're going to surprise him. Matthew 6:8 promises that God knows what we need before we ask him.

You might wonder, then, why it's important to talk to him and to share your heart and your concerns. The thing is, it's not about what you say. It's not about how you say it. It's the fact that every time you pray, you deepen that relationship with God even more. Consider the tree planted by the water. Every time you pray, you dig those roots in a little deeper. You open the door just a little bit more for God to get into your life, your heart, your thoughts, and your actions.

Prayer is the language of a man burdened with a sense of need.

—E. M. Bounds

If we want to become more like Jesus—full of patience, kindness, joy, peace, goodness, and all that other wonderful stuff—we'll do so by spending more time with him. We'll do so by allowing him to pour into us, and allowing ourselves to pour into him.

magic words

There's another thing prayer is not, and that's magic. If you pray for something, it's not automatically going to happen.

In Acts 8, we're told the story of a magician named Simon. He had practiced sorcery for some time, and according to verses 9–10, the Samaritan people were pretty impressed with him. They were so impressed, in fact, that they called him "the Great One—the Power of God." When the magician heard Philip preach, he believed the truth he had heard and was baptized along with the crowds. He was still a little confused, though. When he saw Peter and John lay their hands on others to receive the Holy Spirit, Simon mistakenly thought that he could buy that power for himself.

Peter strongly rebuked Simon in verses 20–23:

May your money perish with you for thinking God's gift can be bought! You can have no part in this, for your heart is not right before God. Turn from your wickedness and pray to the Lord. Perhaps he will forgive your evil thoughts, for I can see that you are full of bitterness and held captive by sin.

Some people think that if you just pray a certain way, everything will come together—just like magic. But that's not the case at all. God is not a puppet on a string, not some cosmic bellhop, waiting for you to tell him where to go or what to do next.

Consider this analogy. A boy is in a candy store with his parents. He's looking this way and that, asking for absolutely everything he sees. From his perspective, it all looks like good stuff. From his parents' viewpoint, it's not. They know, from past experience, what will happen if little Johnny eats every single piece of candy in sight. He'll end up with a stomachache and rotten teeth. The parents see things from a different vantage, through the eyes of experience and wisdom. It's the same way with God. He knows what would happen if he gave us every little thing we wanted or asked for—and he knows the result could be much worse than a mouth full of cavities.

> There are moments when, whatever be the attitude of the body, the soul is on its knees.
>
> —Victor Hugo

The Bible tells us in 2 Corinthians 1:20 that all the promises God made have been fulfilled through Christ. Notice, however, that we're the ones who must add the "amen." Amen basically means "So be it." It's agreeing with God and actively requesting his intervention. Prayer is not just a list of things we want; it is actually a means to partner with God in his work. God chooses to work through us, and it's our choice whether or not we'll partner with him in return.

As we partner more and more with God in his work, we'll notice that it turns out well when we do. We'll begin to depend on that connection with God more and more for our everyday lives, and we'll start to seek God's guidance and counsel earlier in situations that might otherwise puzzle us.

Of course, this goes counter to what society would tell us to do. Society would have us rely on ourselves, on our own wisdom and strength.

going against the flow

Take a look at Ezekiel 47, where the prophet described what he prophetically saw as a Temple. This was an encouragement for the Jewish people who had been in exile for twenty-five years. He told them about the Temple that would be rebuilt; he was trying to help them believe that the land they had been forced out of would once again be theirs.

There was a river flowing out of that Temple, one with strength and depth. In verse 8, we learn that the river had unusual characteristics: It flowed uphill through the desert. First of all, how many times do you find rivers in the desert? And second, when have you ever seen a river that flowed uphill?

The river that's coming from the Temple, from the church, is going uphill, against the grain of what everybody expects. Why would it be a surprise, then, that walking closely with God— talking to him and listening to him—might also go against the grain of what everybody expects?

There is a vast difference between saying prayers and praying.

—Author Unknown

A woman named Esther went against the norms of society. She risked disobeying the law that said no one could go before the king unless summoned. She did so for her people, and ultimately saved them. Then there was Stephen, one of the first persons ever elected to leadership in the church. One day he stepped out, and against the rocks that were being pelted at him, stood firm for what he believed in. Approximately five hundred years ago, there was Martin Luther, who found the boldness to stand before King Charles V. He refused to repent for speaking out about the ways the indulgent church was leading people astray.

A man with God is always in the majority.
—John Knox

God might also call you to take a stand against something that's not right. He might use you to set a new kind of peer pressure in a new direction. On the other hand, he might give you peace exactly where you are, no matter what your circumstance. All of these things will come through prayer.

Connecting to God through prayer provides access to the strength of that uphill-flowing river. It means we have God's ear and access to his heart. God is always patient with us, ready to listen, and willing to give that word of encouragement or direction. All we have to do is be willing to hear it.

dive in

- *Do I really believe that God wants to have a conversation with me?*
- *What would life be like if I talked to God the way I talk to my closest friends?*
- *What would be the best time of day for me to consistently talk to God?*

chapter 10
line of communication

Have you ever known someone who doesn't pray? Some people don't. They think prayer is all about asking, and they feel uncomfortable asking God to concern himself with them. That's just wrong!

So why should we pray? A simple answer is that God commands us to. We're told in Philippians 4:6: "This is what I want you to do: Don't worry about anything. Just pray about everything." Tell God what you need, thank him for all he's done, and you'll experience his peace. Remember, prayer is about relationship. God commands us to pray because, more than anything, he wants us to be in relationship with him.

Have you ever noticed how many times Jesus uses the words "when you pray" in the Bible? He doesn't say, "if you pray," or "should you feel like praying." Jesus says "when." There's an unspoken assumption that prayer would be something you would already know to do. In his case, since he was separated from God's full presence while a man here on earth, Jesus knew that prayer was his life-or-death, essential connection to his Father. You can understand, then, how he would think others would feel the same way. But do we? Do we really see prayer as that life-or-death, essential connection?

Consider this perspective. Let's say you're a parent. What if, for the month of November, you decided not to speak to your children? You just didn't say a word to them for the entire month. How do you think they would feel? Do you think they might begin to question whether or not you really love them?

What about your spouse? What if you decided not to speak to your spouse for a whole month? What do you think that would do to your relationship? Do you think your spouse would still believe that you cared?

This concept easily extends to God. If you chose not to talk to him for a week, a month, or a year, how do you think he'd feel? Do you think God would still believe that you really wanted a relationship with him?

I went to a high school reunion, where I hadn't seen most of the people in thirty years. I could visit with them for a little while and talk about a few things. However, since I don't talk to them very often, there was not much of a relationship present. There was a limit to how far the conversation would go.

On the other hand, my wife and I talk all the time. We have a relationship.

I have a relationship with God. Prayer allows us to develop an intimate relationship with him. Note that I said, "allow." It's all about choosing that relationship, and choosing God, too. When we pray, we're given an opportunity to participate with God in his work.

get a clue

You see, when you get right down to it, my life is not designed for me to just do whatever I want to do. Our lives are designed so that, when we discover what God is doing and what he wants us to do with him, we can begin to find joy, happiness, and purpose. Jesus said in John 14:12 that, "Anyone who believes in me will do the same works I have done, and even greater works." All we have to do is believe, and we're in the game.

> ## If we know how to pray, we know how to live.
>
> **—E. Stanley Jones**

God invites us to do his work. Through prayer, we discover what that work is. Maybe there's someone in our life whom God wants us to reach out to. Maybe there's a mission trip he wants us to go on, or there's someone who could really use a word of encouragement from us. Through prayer, we can be God's hands and feet on earth.

God cares

Prayer also allows us to experience God's love and concern for ourselves. When I pray, I discover just how much God loves me and how much he cares. In Hebrews 4:16, we're told: "Let us come boldly to the throne of our gracious God. There we will receive his mercy, and we will find grace to help us when we need it." The best way to improve self-esteem and figure out who you really are is through prayer. All of a sudden, God will say, "Let me show you how much I love you. Let me show you how much I care for you."

In Luke 11:2, while teaching his followers how to pray, Jesus said, "This is how you should pray: 'Father.'" The word "Father" here actually translates to *Abba*, which means "Daddy." He's telling us, in essence, to regard our relationship with God with that same intimacy, innocence, and tenderness. God, however, is a daddy like the world has never known. This is a daddy who *always* has your best interest at heart and who sees you for who you really are, without you having to explain yourself. This daddy created you and knew you even before you were born.

Do you know what God, as your heavenly Father, really thinks about you? A lot of people grow up never hearing anything good about themselves. They may be under the close scrutiny of parents or others who constantly tell them how wrong they are or how bad they are. God is not like that.

You don't have to be afraid of coming into God's presence because he thinks you're precious (see Isaiah 43:4). You're precious to God for a number of reasons. First, because he created you, and when he did, he made you different from anyone else he'd ever created. There is no one on the face of the earth like you. You are so uniquely created by God that no one else in the world has your DNA, no one else in the world has your thumb print. You are that precious and special to God. Out of billions and billions of people, there is no one like you.

He also says that he has redeemed us. Our nature is like that of Adam. We sin and reject God, but he has redeemed us anyway. The Bible says that God sent his son into the world, and he lived and died in order that we might have life.

> **Too many people overvalue what they are not and undervalue what they are.**
>
> **—Malcolm S. Forbes**

Amazing, isn't it? Can you imagine sacrificing the thing that means the most to you—your very child—for someone else? Can you imagine doing so for someone who might even curse you, or deny you exist? That's the very thing God did. He chose to put us first. As he says in Isaiah 43:1, "I have ransomed you; I have called you by name. You are mine."

One of my favorite verses in the Bible is Isaiah 49:16. I suggest that you write it down, because you can build your life on it. God said, "I have written your name on my hand." When God is in heaven and looks at the palm of his hand, he sees your name on it. That's how precious you are to him. You're not just a number.

> **Man is born broken.**
> **He lives by mending.**
> **The grace of God is glue.**
>
> **—Eugene O'Neill**

You're so precious to God that he has promised to be with you, no matter what you go through. One of the ways you can know he's with you is through prayer.

receive guidance

A father and daughter were taking a walk when they came upon a long, covered bridge. The little girl had never seen one before. As they stepped up to the bridge, she saw that it was totally dark inside, with just a small light at the other end.

She said, "Daddy, I'm scared. I'm not going in there. It's dark."

Her father replied, "I'll tell you what. Let's just start walking toward the light, and the closer we get to it, the brighter that light will become."

That's exactly what God does for us. Through prayer, through relationship with him, he leads us closer and closer toward his light, the place where we don't have to be afraid any more.

God also uses prayer to give us direction for our lives because he has a purpose for each and every one of us. He wants us each to grow to our full potential and to use our abilities to bless others. He helps us find the places we fit, where we're both satisfied and yet challenged. He's just waiting for us to ask for his guidance.

keeping good company

For all the wisdom and guidance God can provide, however, there's something special in the fact that he's even willing to listen to us at all. The Bible tells us over and over in Psalm 37:23, Isaiah 62:4, 2 Chronicles 9:8, and 1 Kings 10:9 that he delights in us, just as we delight in being with those we love.

Some time ago, friends of mine attended a World Congress on Evangelism in Manila. Pastor George Chen from China spoke there. He had been imprisoned in a Chinese prison camp for decades. His captors told him that all he had to do for freedom was renounce his Christian faith. The man refused; he stood by the One he loved.

Early each morning, the prisoner was taken to a raw sewage pit where the captors gave him a shovel and set him to work. Day after day, he shoveled the raw sewage into a ravine so it could be carried away.

> I love the rule and ceremonies of the Church. But I see, well-pleased, that our great Lord can work without them.
>
> —John Wesley

Instead of complaining, however, George Chen realized that it was his chance to spend uninterrupted time with God. While recounting his experience, he made a powerful statement: *"Joy comes in who you're with, not in what the circumstances are."*

We all seem to be trying to improve our circumstances, but the truth is that we'll never find any lasting joy in that. In the midst of that cesspool, Pastor Chen said he used to sing that old hymn that says when you walk with him and talk with him, he tells you that you're his own. He reminds you how very much he loves you.

Understand, though, that God's love for us isn't conditional; it doesn't depend on how much time we actually spend with him. I can guarantee that the more time you spend with him, the more time you're going to want to spend with him. You will keep realizing, over and over, that God loves you and wants you. The cross his Son died on reminds us that, no matter what we do, God still loves us. He still loves us beyond the bounds of human reason. And all we have to do is talk with him.

So why not have a conversation right now? Whether this will be your first real prayer or your ten thousandth, it will still apply. Please read this prayer aloud.

God, thank you for creating me. And thank you for knowing me. Thank you for writing my name on the very palm of your hand, and for remembering me day after day after day.

While you've got his ear, thank God for what he thinks of you, too. Even if you disagree or sometimes think that he made a mistake. Even if you think it's just not worth it, because he obviously thinks it is.

dive in

- *What do I really believe God thinks of me?*
- *How could prayer change the way I think about myself?*
- *What could hinder my ability to have an active, fruitful prayer life?*

God speaks in the silence of the heart.
Listening is the beginning of prayer.

—Mother Teresa

chapter 11

scenario for prayer

A young preacher attended a meeting with several other preachers, and he happened to sit down right next to the bishop. Word had just been received that an afternoon speaker had missed his plane, and couldn't arrive in time for the upcoming event. The bishop turned to the young preacher and said, "Boy, you're an answer to prayer. We just lost our two o'clock speaker, so I want you to fill his place."

The young man replied, "Whoa, sir! I can't do that! I'm not prepared. I don't have any notes."

The bishop replied, "Look, just pray and trust God, and he'll provide."

When the meeting adjourned for lunch, the young man went down to the front pew of the chapel to pray. As he sat down and bowed his head, he looked over and noticed that there was a manila folder laying next to him. He opened it and found a sermon inside. It was a *good* sermon. The young man spent his entire lunch hour learning it. Then, at the appointed time, he preached that powerful sermon to the whole group.

Afterward, though, the bishop ran up to him. "Son, what were you doing? That was my sermon, and I was going to preach it tonight. Now, I don't have anything to preach. What am I going to do?"

What do you think was the young preacher's response? "Bishop, just pray and trust God, and he'll provide."

All humor aside, there's a great truth in that story. If we're willing to pray and trust God, he will provide.

prayer list

While prayer is a conversation with God, sometimes it can be awkward to get a conversation started. So, here's a simple pattern for prayer that my father, who is a preacher, taught me. It's very easy to remember, and you'll be reminded of it every time you look at your hands.

We have to pray with our eye on God, not on the difficulties.

—Oswald Chambers

First of all, look at your thumb. This is the finger that's closest to us, so it represents those that are nearest to us. The list might include your parents, spouse, children, best friend . . . you get the idea. Every day, pray for them that God would meet their needs, guide, and direct them; that they would be aware of God's presence in their lives; or whatever you think is appropriate.

Next is the pointing finger. If you want to designate something in particular, you use that finger to point to it. That finger represents those who point us to Christ. My father taught me to pray for our preacher every day. Pray for the chairman of your church board. Pray for the other leaders. While you're at it, let them know you're praying for them. I'm certain they'll be glad to hear it.

The third finger is the tallest. That one stands for people in high places. When we pray, we need to remember our president and his family, as well as our senators, congressional leaders, mayors, and others in government. We can ask God to give them wisdom, to help them clearly see the answers they're looking for, and to lead us in a way that glorifies the Lord.

The fourth finger is the weakest one. Let that finger remind us to pray for those around us who are weak, whether they're sick, hospitalized, or going through financial or emotional tough times. Whatever the need, God can help.

listen closely

My father has had a ministry to alcoholics for a long time, and he's been blessed to be able to help some of them get beyond their challenges. He tells of a young man in his twenties, who lived in a nearby town. My dad spent a lot of time with him. The man had been addicted to alcohol, but had finally overcome his habit and hadn't touched a drop for about six or eight months.

One Saturday morning about nine o'clock, my father found himself in the parking lot of the church in his friend's town. All of a sudden, a pickup truck came around the corner and pulled up right beside him. He realized the driver was the young man, who invited my dad to get into the truck.

When he got in, there was a six-pack of beer on the seat. He asked the guy what was going on.

The young man said, "I woke up this morning at six o'clock, so nervous I couldn't be still. I just had to have a drink. I couldn't control myself. But I thought of you." The young man pointed out, "I don't know if you know it or not, but the Lord had you standing in the middle of this parking lot on a Saturday morning. Do you do that every Saturday?" My dad answered no.

The man said, "The Lord had you here this morning. If you hadn't been here, I'd have been drunk in another hour. Thank God, you're here. Thank you that you're here."

We need to be aware that there are people around us who need us, just like that young man needed my dad that day. There are so many out there who need a helping hand, a word of encouragement, or just to know that someone else cares enough about them to lift them up in prayer.

Finally, there's that little finger on my hand—and there's a reason we come to it last. My own little finger represents me. My dad taught me that, after I've prayed for those who are close to me, who lead my church, who hold other positions of authority, and those who are weak, then I can pray for myself.

Pray, and let God worry.

—Martin Luther

An interesting thing happens when we pray like this. It might seem like we'd get to ourselves and our own needs quickly, but once we get into that conversation with God, we start remembering all the other people around us who really need something first. When we pray for other people, we see them in a different light, and we see our own lives in a different light, as well.

motivation

No matter who we pray for—whether it's ourselves or someone else—it's important that we do so with right motives. In 1 John 5:14–17, we're told:

We can be confident that he will listen to us whenever we ask him for anything in line with his will. And if we know he is listening when we make our requests, we can be sure that he will give us what we ask for.

The question is, then, how do we know if what we're asking is in line with God's will? How do we know that we're asking with the right motives? The simple answer is that the better we know God, the more certain we can be of his will. When we spend time with him in prayer and reading the Bible, we learn more about the things that are important to him. Things like putting others before ourselves, living lives that honor him, and doing our best to be good representatives of him here on earth. We also learn to ask God what his will is in certain situations, understanding from experience that he really does know best, and then we can line up our desires to match that will.

attitude

It's also important that we pray with an attitude of thanksgiving. Look at what Paul wrote in Colossians 4:2–6: "Devote yourself to prayer with an alert mind and a thankful heart."

A member of our congregation recently had a particular problem in her life, and some of her friends asked if she had ever thanked God for that problem. She admitted she hadn't, but decided to give it a try. She began thanking God for the problem and for the opportunities for growth it represented. Before long, God showed her why she had the problem and how it could be used.

We can become so busy complaining about our problems that we aren't thankful for the opportunities they provide. There are so many things we can be thankful for. "No matter what happens," we're told in 1 Thessalonians 5:18, "always be thankful. For this is God's will for you who belong to Jesus Christ."

persistence

It's also God's desire that we pray persistently. In Matthew 7:7, Jesus instructed us: "Keep on asking, and you will be given what you ask for. Keep on looking, and you will find. Keep on knocking, and the door will be opened."

There's a great illustration of this in Luke 18:1–8. Jesus told his disciples about a judge "who was a godless man with great contempt for everyone." A widow was seeking justice against someone who had harmed her, so she went to the judge again and again with her story.

The value of consistent prayer
is not that he will hear us,
but that we will hear him.

—William McGill

For a while, the judge simply ignored her. Finally, though, enough was enough. "'I fear neither God nor man,' he says to himself, 'but this woman is driving me crazy. I'm going to see that she gets justice, because she is wearing me out with her constant requests!'"

Jesus instructed:

Learn a lesson from this evil judge. Even he rendered a just decision in the end, so don't you think God will surely give justice to his chosen people who plead with him day and night? Will he keep putting them off? I tell you, he will grant justice to them quickly!

If you've been praying for something and you haven't yet seen that prayer answered, have you allowed yourself to get sidetracked, discouraged, and despondent? Or are you still praying with persistence?

I once heard about a man who became a Christian in his late seventies; in fact, he was led to Christ the week before he died. His family had been praying for him for forty years. Yes, forty years. And that prayer was answered. How many of us are willing to keep praying for something for that long?

Let's face it, most of us are pretty impatient. We want what we want, when we want it. We expect God to do it now or we move on to something else.

Remember, though, God has a perfect time for answering our prayers. While we're praying, he's busy behind the scenes pulling everything else together so those prayers are answered in just the right way.

Here's where the element of trust comes into play. If we're asking with the right motives, a thankful heart, and persistence, God will take care of the rest.

dive in
- *How has prayer helped me see someone else—or myself—in a different light?*
- *What stands in the way of me being more persistent with my prayers?*
- *Am I more likely to pray for God's will or my own?*

I have been driven many times to my knees
by the overwhelming conviction that I had nowhere else to go.
—Abraham Lincoln

standing in the gap

The great writer W. Somerset Maugham wove the traits of his friends (without revealing their identities) into the characters in his stories. After he had written several stories, Maugham noticed something. Whenever he incorporated a friend's good, noble qualities into a character for one of his stories, nobody recognized who provided the inspiration. By contrast, every time Maugham placed a problem, fault, or defect into a fictional character, people immediately knew about whom he was speaking. Maugham said that he discovered: "We know our friends by their defects rather than their merits."

It's sad to say, but it's true. We, as a society, are so quick to tear each other down that it's no wonder so many people struggle with issues of self-esteem. A 1986 survey by the Institute of Family Relations showed that mothers criticized their children ten times for every one time they said something positive. We're talking about mothers here. How much worse can it get?

As Christians, however, we have an opportunity to undo some of the damage that's been done. We can make a difference when we build each other up through prayer.

on behalf of others

The Bible calls prayer for others "standing in the gap," and the reference comes from Ezekiel 22:30. According to the prophet who wrote the chapter, the walls of righteousness that guard the land need repairing, and God is looking for someone who is willing to stand in the gap in the walls for others who aren't able.

> We can do no great things,
> only small things with great love.
> —Mother Teresa

One year around Christmastime, two brothers decided to visit their neighbor. A pond separated their house and the neighbor's. Since it was frozen over, the father said they could walk across it. He sat on the porch with his binoculars to watch and make sure they would be all right.

Along the way, the boys came across a crack in the ice. Their father intently watched as the thirteen-year-old knelt down by the crack. He put his knees on one side of the crack and his hands on the other, and then told his three-year-old brother to walk across his back so he'd be safe. It was a beautiful thing.

We stand in the gap when we're willing to put ourselves in the middle of a problem and then let people walk over us to get to where they need to be. We become connecting conduits, something the world needs a lot more these days.

This praying for others can be very powerful, and it is needed. It's important to pray specifically for two overall groups: the people in our church and the people outside of it.

inside

Let's start with the people in our own congregations. People ask me all the time how they should stand in the gap for the church as a whole. Praying for unity in our church is so very, very important. Our unity makes other people sit up and take notice. When we're all unified and going in the same direction, we have unbelievable power to overcome the enemy and to do God's work here on earth.

Another thing to pray for is boldness in the church. Our priority, as Christians, is to win people to Christ, to "go and make disciples of all the nations," as we're commanded in Matthew 28:19. Many unchurched people will cross paths with the members of my church this very week. So what are we going to do about it? Are we going to be bold and share how much God loves them? Are we going to take the time to pray that others in the congregation will be bold, as well?

Third, we need to pray that we would not forget where we came from while we're trying to get where we're going. Everything we have has been made possible by the people who have come before us, so it's important to thank God for them. We're reminded in Deuteronomy 6:10–12 that the promised land will be filled with prosperous cities that we didn't build.

> The houses will be richly stocked with goods you did not produce. You will draw water from cisterns you did not dig, and you will eat from vineyards and olive trees you did not plant.

When we have eaten our fill in that land, we must be careful not to forget the Lord, who prepared the way and brought us here.

Pray also that, as a church, we will abide in God's presence. People tend to think that God's going to be in the actual church building. God may be in the building, but he's bigger than the building. As the author of 2 Chronicles 2:6 asked, "Who can really build him a worthy home? Not even the highest heavens can contain him!"

God is everywhere, and we carry him with us. Let's pray that we're always aware of that fact, just as David was. In Psalm 139:7–10, he exclaimed:

> I can never escape from your spirit!
> I can never get away from your presence!
> If I go up to heaven, you are there;
>   if I go down to the place of the dead, you are there.
> If I ride the wings of the morning,
>   if I dwell by the farthest oceans,
>   even there your hand will guide me,
>   and your strength will support me.

We can also pray for the willingness to ask for God's pardon, and that the church would be a place where anybody in the community would feel comfortable enough to come in and ask for God's pardon, too. The church is not just a building or a list of programs. It's a place where people come to get right with God. It's a gathering of imperfect folks, sinners who come seeking God's forgiveness by his grace.

The church is only the church when it is there for others.

—Dietrich Bonhoeffer

We can also pray that we learn to accept God's provision. After all, God always provides us with what we need. When he calls us to a certain task, he gives whatever we will need to accomplish it. Our own doubts and fears can get in the way of believing that. For example, Moses began to worry that he had no way to feed the huge group of people he was leading out of Egypt. In Exodus 16:3, Moses even accused God of bringing them into the desert so they would starve to death.

God told Moses in the next verse that he was going to rain down food from heaven for them. Then the people could go out each day and pick up as much food as needed. In essence, he told Moses, "You do your part, and I'll do mine."

Let's pray that, whatever God calls us to do, we will be willing to do our part and trust that he will do his. May we accept his provision, however it comes. If I had been Moses, I think I would have asked God to consider giving the people a few days' worth of food at a time, so I could show them what was happening. Or I would have wanted a freezer to store some up for later. But that's not how God works. He didn't provide any more food than they needed at the time they needed it.

Right now, there are people in the church who are dealing with things that they just don't think they can handle. Pray that they—that we—would be willing to let God provide whatever will make the difference.

It's important that we also pray that we'll advance God's purpose—that all the people of the earth would come to know him (see 1 Kings 8:43).

Paul put it this way in Philippians 2:10–11:

> At the name of Jesus every knee will bow, in heaven and on earth and under the earth, and every tongue will confess that Jesus Christ is Lord, to the glory of God the Father.

As a church, there are many ways we can do this: invite people to worship services with us, share our testimonies, and we can pray that the people who don't know God would believe.

outside

We must also pray for those outside the church. We can pray that their hearts would be open to truth and that they would cross the paths of Christians willing to share with them. We can pray that the walls that have kept them from accepting God's gracious love for them would be torn down.

In Genesis 18, we find the story of how Abraham stood in the gap for a couple of places called Sodom and Gomorrah. The people in those two areas were extremely evil, and everything they did was wicked, so God threatened to destroy them.

Abraham questioned God in verse 23: "Will you destroy both innocent and guilty alike? Suppose you find fifty innocent people there within the city—will you still destroy it, and not spare it for their sakes?" God replied that if he could find fifty innocent people in Sodom, he would spare the whole city.

Abraham still wasn't satisfied. He asked again, what if there were only forty-five, or forty, or thirty, or twenty, or ten?

Finally, God promised that even if there were only ten innocent people in the whole city, he wouldn't destroy it.

Courage is not the absence of fear, but rather the judgment that something else is more important than fear.

—Ambrose Redmoon

There's no telling how many lives Abraham's pleas affected. His example is such a strong one to follow. Abraham put himself on the line to save innocent lives. He was willing to stand in the gap. Through our prayers for others, we can do the same.

God is still looking for people who are willing to build up walls rather than tear them down, who are willing to be sensitive to others and aware of their needs. When he looks among us, will he find one?

dive in

- *What kind of things can prevent me from praying for my church?*
- *How often do I pray for people outside the church?*
- *In the grand scheme of things, why are my individual prayers important?*

Trouble and perplexity drive me to prayer,
and prayer drives away perplexity and trouble.
—*Philipp Melanchthon*

chapter 13

products of prayer

Wherever you are today, look up at the ceiling.

Sometimes, when people have been praying but they haven't seen the answers yet, they say their prayers are bouncing off that ceiling.

Now, ceilings are an important part of any house. They help with the structure, hold the walls in place, and separate the rooms from the attic. But there's one thing they can't do, and that's contain your prayers—or your relationship with God.

When you pray, there's a lot more happening than meets the eye. Just because you haven't seen God respond in the way you want or expect him to yet, it doesn't mean you're just praying for nothing. It doesn't mean God just hasn't gotten around to you yet. Remember, as it says in Acts 10:34, that God "doesn't show partiality," so your prayers are every bit as important to him as anyone else's.

In the tenth chapter of Daniel, there's a story that helps us see what's happening behind the scenes. The prophet Daniel had a vision and had been praying for the ability to understand it for weeks on end. At the same time, we're told in verse 2, he was partially fasting and mourning.

Finally, an angel appeared to Daniel, and this is what he said:

> Don't be afraid, Daniel. Since the first day you began to pray for understanding and to humble yourself before your God, your request has been heard in heaven. I have come in answer to your prayer. But for twenty-one days the spirit prince of the kingdom of Persia blocked my way. Then Michael, one of the archangels, came to help me, and I left him there with the spirit prince of the kingdom of Persia. Now I am here to explain what will happen to your people in the future, for this vision concerns a time yet to come.

The answers to our prayers sometimes face opposition. We know that we have a very real enemy, Satan, who wants to keep us from connecting with God. But God is more powerful. So, if we're willing to keep praying, to keep knocking, and to keep seeking, we're going to see prayers come to pass. Along the way, we'll also see changes in ourselves and our surroundings, because there's no way we can come into God's presence and go away unchanged.

confession

One of the things that happens when we pray is that confession takes place. It's only natural. We see how awesome and powerful God is, and in that light, we realize how frail and human we are.

Jesus told a story in Luke 18:10–14 about two men who went to the Temple to pray. One of them, according to the story, was an overly proud man, and the other one was a tax collector. Now, in that time, tax collectors weren't very well thought of, so the proud man considered himself in better standing. When he prayed, according to verse 11, he actually said:

Thank you, God, that I am not a sinner like everyone else, especially like that tax collector over there! For I never cheat, I don't sin, I don't commit adultery, I fast twice a week, and I give you a tenth of my income.

The tax collector, on the other hand, "stood at a distance and dared not even lift his eyes to heaven as he prayed. Instead, he beat his chest in sorrow, saying, 'O God, be merciful to me, for I am a sinner.'" And only that sinner, Jesus said, returned home justified before God. "For the proud will be humbled, but the humble will be honored."

> God grant me the serenity to accept the people I cannot change, the courage to change the one I can, and the wisdom to know it's me.
>
> **—Author Unknown**

When faith really means something to people, they're not afraid to come into the awesome power of God, to stand in awe, to see themselves as they really are, and to admit that they're not perfect. Psychologists tell us that the three hardest words for an individual to say are "I am wrong." We'd rather be right than be president, and we don't really want to confess. We form all sorts of theories to justify the things we've done. But instead, what we ought to do is just bow and confess. And the more we pray, the more we see how much of a relief it is, and the easier it gets.

change

There's another thing that happens when we pray, and that's change. Confession always brings change.

An old farmer and his wife lived in the hills. The farmer said, "Ma, we gotta go to town once before we die." So they went.

The town had a nice new hotel. Neither of them had ever seen a hotel, much less been in one. They stepped into the lobby and happened to stand next to an elevator. The elevator door opened, so the woman, being faster than her husband, stepped inside to see what was going on. The door suddenly closed and she just disappeared.

About forty-five seconds went by, and much to the farmer's surprise, the door opened again, and off stepped a beautiful young lady.

He went up and hugged her, and said, "Ma, I don't know where you've been or what they did, but we ought to have come to town a long time ago!"

When you are through changing, you are through.

—Bruce Barton

When we pray, confess, and finally see change come, we might wonder why it took us so long to get to town, too.

community

Prayer isn't just an individual thing. It also brings community. When people come together to pray, encourage, and love one another, there's unity. We learn that we can trust each other with our burdens and share in each other's joys.

People hunger to be part of a community, a real fellowship. They're looking for a safe place, and when the church comes together in unity, we can be that safe place. It doesn't matter where we're from or what we've done. We're just sinners who have been saved by grace, and that makes us all welcome to come receive forgiveness and be part of the community. The ground is always level at the foot of the cross. Prayer helps us realize that, and helps us find just the place where we fit in.

conformity

Prayer also brings conformity. I don't mean it turns us into cookie-cutter versions of ourselves, where everyone is exactly the same. I mean it brings conformity to God's will. It's not always an easy process, but it will happen regardless. Even Jesus struggled with this. In Luke 22, it says he knew the Roman soldiers were on their way to seize him, so he stepped aside to pray alone. Verse 41 tells us that Jesus knelt down and prayed, "Father, if you are willing, please take this cup of suffering away from me. Yet I want your will, not mine."

What happened next? "An angel from heaven appeared and strengthened him." When we get to the point that we're willing to say, "God, your will is more important than mine," God helps us out. God helps us conform to his will.

A lot of people really struggle with questions about what's right and what's wrong. We can conform to what the world says is right, or we can conform to what God's Word says. That's our choice. And I'll tell you what: You can have all the ambition there is while you're climbing that ladder of success, but when you get to the top, you might find that the ladder is leaning against the wrong building. God has something for us that's bigger and better than we can imagine, and we receive it by conforming to his will.

If we allow him to, God will show us the next rung of the ladder as we go. He'll help us take one step at a time, and with him as our guide, we'll be able to reach the heights he has for us. Ignoring his direction, however, can mean a lot of wasted effort. It shows that our priorities are a little off, and that we may rely on our own strength and understanding a little too much.

Let's say my wife is standing on a pier, and I'm out in a boat. If I throw a rope over to her while she's on that pier, I don't pull the pier out to the boat. No, she takes the rope and pulls the boat into the pier, because the pier is the part that's secure. It's the same thing with prayer. We can't pull God to where we want him to be.

Instead, through submission, he pulls us to where he wants us to be according to his will, and that place is a whole lot more secure.

I'm not saying it's always easy to submit, but it is essential. I know a story about a man on a battleship. One night, he saw flashing lights ahead that were right in his path. He sent a message saying, "Change your course ten degrees south." In a minute, he had a response, which said, "No, *you* change your course ten degrees north."

> ## What good is having someone who can walk on water if you don't follow in his footsteps?
> **—Author Unknown**

He was a little irritated by this, so he said to his subordinate, "Send a message back saying I'm the captain of this ship and to change ten degrees south." This time, the return message said, "I'm a seaman first class, but *you* need to change your course ten degrees north."

By now, the captain was infuriated. He said, "Wire back and say we're a battleship, and we're coming through. Change ten degrees south." The reply? "*You* change ten degrees north. I'm a lighthouse, and I'm staying put."

Sometimes the more rank we get, the more we think we know about God's will. As a pastor, I sometimes have to be reminded of this. When you're in full-time ministry, you tend to think you know more about God's will than some other people. But God also says to me, just as much as anyone else, "Hey, I'm the lighthouse, and I'm staying put. You need to conform your ways to mine."

commissioning

When people pray, there's another thing that occurs: commissioning. Prayer allows us to receive our instructions so we'll be ready to move out and do what God has for us to do. When you and I pray—and we pray more than just "gimme, gimme"—we learn about God's will for our lives. We are reminded of others whose lives we can touch and situations in which we can make a positive difference. We confess, we change, we find community, we conform to God's will, and we're commissioned to serve him.

dive in

- *How does prayer change me?*
- *What's the biggest challenge for me when it comes to conforming to God's will?*
- *When have I seen prayer help strengthen the community around me?*

*Every tomorrow has two handles. We can take hold of it
by the handle of anxiety or by the handle of faith.*
—*Author Unknown*

chapter 14
praying with power

P rayer is really such a simple concept. We talk to God and God talks to us. And perhaps most important, God listens to us and we listen to God. It all comes down to the fact that prayer really is as simple as conversation. Maybe you're thinking, "I don't do small talk well." That doesn't matter. God isn't bored by our feeble attempts at carrying on a conversation, and he doesn't criticize the way we say things. He's happy just to be with us.

Of course, there are some specific things that God has told us to do when we pray and ways he's told us not to pray. Somehow, though, many of us have forgotten that, and we've tried to make it difficult. We've tried to create all sorts of rules for what prayer should look like and how it's done. I'm not talking about rules—rules Jesus told us to do and not to do in praying. No, I mean that some of us have created a long list of dos and don'ts regarding prayer . . . creating a doctrine, as it were. And that's not what it's really about.

All those rules only serve to keep us from praying. We end up thinking we don't measure up, or we haven't jumped through enough hoops to make ourselves worthy to come into God's presence. The truth is, we can't do anything to make ourselves worthy to have an audience with the King of the universe, so we shouldn't even try. God accepts us anyway.

Don't think, though, that if prayer is easy, it must not be important. Prayer is the power behind our Christian walk. We may want someone to come to know Jesus, and we may witness to them all we want. However, unless we combine that with prayer, it's not likely to happen. It's our prayers that allow God to work on the heart, not our words that work on the ear. If we truly understood just how powerful prayer could be, we'd do much more of it.

Never forget that prayer can move mountains, heal the sick, bind wounds, set captives free, calm storms, and even bring the dead back to life. All this and more is available for the asking, and yet, it's all too easy for us to take it for granted.

So, what is the condition of your prayer life? Are you invigorated by remembering how much power is available through it? Have you been challenged by how much untapped power you have? Let's review:

tapping into the source

In the heat of summer months, we often have to water our plants. Giving a plant too little water, though, can be worse than not watering it at all. This is because if we only wet the surface, the plant's roots begin to draw closer to the surface to get a drink of that refreshing water. When the roots are close to the surface, the plant struggles more when the next day's sun beats down. Ultimately, this can be fatal to a young plant. It is vital to take the time to water a plant long, slowly, and thoroughly, allowing the roots to be refreshed deep down in the soil.

Where are your roots right now? Have you only wet the surface during your conversations with God? If so, your roots will be more susceptible the next time you hit a spiritual drought. If you have watered your spirit consistently and forced your roots deeper into the soil, then you will be much more stable when you face challenges.

What does your vegetation show to people looking for signs of water? Do you look tired and withered like the rest of the world? Are you wilted and desperate for a satisfying drink? Or is your life lush and fruitful? Do you show signs of having been watered by your time with the Lord?

How much water have I had this week?

prayer defined

Because prayer is really a two-way conversation between us and God, there's no magic formula to it, though there are some ways of helping us remember what to pray. We can pray by using the five fingers as a guide, or we can use the model Jesus provided in the Lord's Prayer (see Matt. 6:9–13).

Consider an appliance that hasn't been plugged into an electrical outlet. Its manual can promise all sorts of lofty ambitions, but there's no way that appliance will ever measure up to those promises with the power turned off. Our spiritual lives can be that way, too, if we aren't plugged into the power source of prayer.

Prayer is a spiritual muscle, strengthened when we use it. We don't improve our physical fitness by reading a book about aerobic activity, and we don't build muscles by talking about how strong we'd like to be. In the same way, prayer is something that we get better at only by doing it.

Have I seen God's hand move in response to my prayers?

line of communication

God created us so that we could be in relationship with him, and he wants to work through us to accomplish his purposes.

When everything else is stripped away, those are the two things that matter most.

Prayer is a conduit to our relationship with God. It's time we share with God and he shares with us. It's time when we get to know each other a little better and time when we get to know just what God thinks of us. If we listen closely enough, he'll tell us those wonderful things.

Prayer is also about partnering together on tasks. Remember that verse in 2 Corinthians 1:20 that says all of God's promises have been fulfilled through Christ, but we are to say the "amen." Since "amen" basically means, "so be it," it's up to us to speak the "so be it" to agree with all of the promises that God has made. Although there can be a lot waiting for us, sometimes God's hand is held back while he's waiting for us to join him in his work.

God could, of course, do anything he wants whether we partner with him or not. He didn't set things up to work that way, though. He set the world up so that we'd have to work with him, and he'd have to work through us, for things to happen.

What is God waiting for me to partner with him to do?

scenario for prayer

Although there are no magic formulas to prayer, there are certain things that we need to do to make our prayers most effective. Most of them have more to do with the condition of our hearts than they do with how we pray.

Not one of us is worthy to come before God unless we begin by confession and by admitting we're unworthy. We need to accept the pardon that God gives. He supplies power in prayer to those who are totally humbled and repentant before him.

If we get our attitude right at the start, then our prayers will be more powerful. The Bible tells us that God will give us anything we ask, when we ask in accordance with his will. But how do we know if we're praying in accordance with his will? Well, we know that anything we find in the Bible is in accordance with his will, so consider starting there. Find the promises of God, and claim them for your own life. Pray for your health, pray for your leaders, pray for the prosperity of the city where you live.

Beyond that, though, the more time we spend with God—in Christian community, in prayer, and in reading the Word—the more likely we are to understand his heart and to pray for those things that line up with his will rather than our own selfish desires. There's a great benefit to that—while we may never literally ask for it when we pray, God uses our prayers to change us. We become most like those we spend time with, after all. Prayer makes us more like God.

We also need to pray with belief that God can accomplish what we ask him to do. To pray without faith is little more than spouting words. Prayer can change that, too. When you need to pray about something but you're overwhelmed by the bigness of it all, start by asking God to change your heart, increase your faith, and show you what to pray. It's amazing what happens when you do this. The problem may not necessarily change, but your perception of it will.

Above all else, we must follow the model of Jesus in the garden of Gethsemane and have the stance that it's "not what I want, but what you want." Do you know why many don't experience the power of prayer? It's because we always try to bend God's will to meet our desires, yet prayer is when God bends our will to meet his. That's the place we discover God's desire and God's practice.

Where does my will need to bend to God's?

standing in the gap

We have power at our disposal, but God never meant it to be used selfishly. The Bible is full of stories of people praying for others. God created us to be dependent on each other, and we are commanded to love one another—prayer is often a way we can achieve this.

Many times, when we see someone else struggling, we want to do whatever we can to help. We often become so caught up in helping in tangible ways, that we forget to help out in the most powerful way: through prayer. God doesn't call us to fill every need we see; but he often burdens us to pray for each other.

Where does God want me to commit to stand in the gap through prayer?

products of prayer

When we bow before God, he puts a concept in our mind of what he wants us to do and to be. The prophet Joel says, "Your sons and daughters will prophesy, your old men will dream dreams, your young men will see visions" (Joel 2:27–29). So come before God and just say, "Now, God, what do you want to show me in my mind's eye?" Do you realize that every great thing that's ever been accomplished started in the mind? Franklin Jacobs broke the world record at the indoor high jump. When people asked how he did it, he replied that he had wanted to in the past, but it wasn't until he actually had a picture in his mind of going over the pole that he could accomplish it.

God may not have a world record for you, nor may he have greatness for you in the way the world imagines greatness. Are you brave enough to ask God to show you the impossible? Are you willing to let him open your mind's eye to see the unthinkable? Are you willing to dream dreams or see visions?

What's in my mind's eye?

part III
jumping in
with both feet

In union there is strength.

—*Aesop*

chapter 15
pulling together

Times were tough in the United States between 1929 and 1933. It was the time of the Great Depression, and the unemployment rate rose from approximately 3 percent to almost 25 percent.

People were desperate for work. They'd do anything to support themselves and their families, so it should come as no surprise that more than five thousand workers moved to the dry, desolate border of Arizona and Nevada to build a dam.

Many workers brought their families, but they suffered with poor sanitary conditions, heat that reached almost 120 degrees, and little clean water in the tent city they shared. They pulled together for a common purpose: constructing Hoover Dam, the largest one in the world at that time. Guided by a team of six construction companies and requiring four and a half years of construction, Hoover Dam was completed in the fall of 1935. It stood 725 feet high, was 1,244 feet wide, and measured 660 feet thick at its base. It was composed of 4.4 million yards of concrete. (It's been said that's enough concrete to pave a sixteen-foot-wide highway from California to New York!)

The dam wasn't built to provide people with employment. Rather, it was a grand plan to harness the power of the Colorado River. That mighty river's flow was uneven. In the spring, it flooded all of the nearby low-lying areas. Then by summer, it all but dried up. The inconsistency didn't help much when it came to irrigation.

Because those people were willing to come together and give it their all, they changed the landscape. All these years later, the effects are still felt. The reservoir of water held by the dam allows farmers to grow crops all year long. That's not all. The water powers seventeen generators that produce enough electricity to keep Southern California, Arizona, and Nevada with light all year.

team work

Let's look at the importance of presence. In other words, committing to show up and be part of a Christian community. Why is that so important?

Think back to that dam. There's no way that the project, as big as it was, could have been done without everyone involved. And we, as Christians, have a big job in front of us, as well. We're called to "go and make disciples of all nations," as it says in Matthew 28:18–20. There's no way we can do that alone.

The thing is, if we're willing to pitch our tents, roll up our sleeves, and get to work, we can change the landscape every bit as much as those construction workers did so many years ago. By showing up and taking part in what's happening, we, too, can help irrigate the land with living water and offer God's power to people far and wide.

For all that to happen, though, there's something that we have to know as individuals. You and I need to understand that church isn't the same when we're not there. We miss something when we're absent, but the church misses out, too.

That's probably why Hebrews 10:25 urges, "Let us not neglect our meeting together, as some people do." God knows that we can't accomplish alone what needs be done.

> **I am of the opinion that my life belongs to the whole community and as long as I live, it is my privilege to do for it whatever I can.**
>
> **—George Bernard Shaw**

As we explore the idea of presence, we're going to talk a lot about the church as a family. By the end of the study, I hope you'll understand the joys of being with that family, and understand the difference between showing up because you're supposed to and showing up because you really want to.

radical obedience

I want to share with you something I once read. Chuck Swindoll talked about a house church meeting in a Communist country. Christians in some countries still need to sneak around to meet; yet we take for granted that we can walk into a church and worship at any time in America.

As the story goes, a group of Christians had come together on a Sunday for worship. They arrived at the house in little groups so they wouldn't make the Communist authorities suspicious.

They were all locked in this house with the doors and windows closed, and they were singing a hymn. Suddenly, two soldiers came bursting through the doors with loaded automatic weapons. One shouted, "All right, everybody line up against the wall. If you wish to renounce your commitment to Jesus Christ, leave now!" A few left, then another, and then a couple more.

The command came again: "This is your last chance. Either turn against your faith in Christ, or stay and suffer the consequences." Several more slipped out, but others didn't move. They had no idea what would happen next. The room was silent.

After a few moments had passed, one of the soldiers closed the door, looked back at the ones who remained, and said, "Keep your hands up, but this time in praise to our Lord Jesus Christ, brothers and sisters. We, too, are Christians. We have learned by experience, however, that unless people are willing to die for their faith, they cannot be fully trusted."

Going to church doesn't make you a Christian any more than going to a garage makes you an automobile.

—Billy Sunday

Talk about a witness. Talk about willing to be present! Of course, we don't live in that kind of atmosphere. We're not worried that soldiers are going to disrupt our worship services and put guns in our faces. Going to church isn't illegal. But when things are easy, we sometimes forget about the commitment that's supposed to go along with them. What if our lives depended on that commitment? What if we were willing to look at it as radical obedience?

keeping commitments

At my church, we take the idea of presence very seriously. In fact, we ask people to write down the number of Sundays they'll attend worship services in the coming year. Now, we don't take roll to see who's there or who's not, but we don't need to. We've found that when people commit to be here, they follow through with what they said they'd do, no matter what.

They know that when they're not at the service, there's no telling what they'll miss, what they would have been able to teach somebody, what they would have learned, how somebody might have encouraged them, or how they might have helped someone else. I'll give you an example.

A dozen or so years ago, a huge ice storm came through our city. It arrived on Friday, and it was looking pretty bad. Most churches in town announced that they wouldn't have services that weekend, because we were all supposed to be iced in for the next several days. At my church, however, we decided not to make that announcement. We decided we'd have church, and if people wanted to come, they'd come. We figured we'd rather take a chance just in case the weather wasn't too severe.

I arrived at church around six thirty that Sunday morning. Ice was everywhere, but I wasn't there alone. One of the first people I saw was an elderly member. I said, "Miss Lucille, I didn't expect to see you here today."

Do you know what she replied? "Why?"

I responded, "Well, it's so icy, and you have to have somebody to drive you, so I thought you'd decide not to come today."

Eighty percent of success is showing up.
—Woody Allen

Boy, did she teach this preacher a lesson. She said, "John Ed, I didn't decide this morning to come today. If I had waited until this morning to decide, I wouldn't have come. It's too cold. But, you see, I decided last November when I turned in my commitment card that I'd be here forty-eight Sundays. I know what four I'm going to be out of town, and this isn't one of them. I decided last November that I'd be here this Sunday in February."

She already knew what so many people eventually find out: If you wait until Sunday morning to decide whether or not you'll go to church, you'll most likely never get there. It'll probably be pretty easy to find an excuse not to go. If you make a commitment that you're part of the family and you're not going to miss an opportunity to take part in whatever happens, however, you'll end up with a much better track record. You—and your church—will be all the better for it.

strategic pauses

A couple of lumberjacks were hard at work. One was an older gentleman, and the other was a young guy. The younger one said to the old man, "I bet I can cut more logs than you can today."

The older one replied, "I bet you can't."

So they went to battle. They set a four-hour time limit, and raced to see who could cut the most logs in that time. The young man went after it, and he didn't stop for that entire four hours. When he was finished he had a pile of logs.

Along the way, every thirty or forty minutes, he'd notice the old man taking a break for a little while. He thought to himself, *That old man's getting tired, and he can't keep up with me. I know I'll win.*

But when the four hours was up, the young man couldn't believe his eyes. The old man had cut twice as many logs as he had.

He looked at him in disbelief, and said, "How did you do that? You kept stopping so often!"

The man replied, "Son, I was sharpening my axe."

So many people resemble that young man, just charging through life. It doesn't have to be that way. If we can learn to come together on a regular basis to "sharpen our axes," there's no telling what we can pull off as a church—as a family.

You know, the workers toiling away on the Hoover Dam got paid. It wasn't entirely a selfless act. In fact, some of them may have been so focused on doing it for the money that they may have missed the grander scheme, or the fact that they were a part of something so much larger than themselves.

I think some people look at church that way, too. They see it as something they do to even things out, to help balance the bad parts of life with the good.

But we have an opportunity to do so much more than just show up. As the family of God, we can commit to building up God's kingdom, no matter what it takes. In the process, we can keep that flow of living water available for generations to come.

dive in

- *If somebody asked me how many Sundays I'd be at church in the next year, what would I say?*
- *How committed would I be to attending worship if I lived somewhere that it had to be done in secret?*
- *What am I likely to miss when I'm not at church?*

God waits to win back his own flowers
as gifts from man's hand.
—Rabindranath Tagore

chapter 16

God our father

I'd like to tell you a story about a dad, probably not that different from the dads of our day, who had two sons. One of his sons came to him one day and said, "I want my share of your estate now, instead of waiting until you die." We don't know what prompted his request, but Luke 15:12 tells us what happened next. That man did what his son asked; he divided his property between his two sons.

The son who made the request gathered together all he had, then set off for a foreign land. Once he got there, he "wasted all his money on wild living" (Luke 15:13). When it was all spent, he found himself in need. He was so desperate that he longed to eat even the food the pigs were eating. So desperate, in fact, that he finally came to his senses and decided to go home.

The young man didn't consider himself worthy of even being treated like a servant in his father's house when he returned, much less a son. There's something he didn't count on; he didn't figure a father's love into the equation.

You know the rest of the story. When the father saw his son coming, he was filled with compassion and ran to meet him with open arms. Luke 15:20 tells us that the father saw him approaching from "a long distance away." He must have been waiting, watching, hoping that one day his son would come back. That day, he did.

The father, at this point, didn't care what he had done; all that mattered was that his son had returned. A celebration was in order.

family matters

There's just something about family that's different than friends or acquaintances. Now, I realize that not everyone has had the perfect family experience, and sometimes your relatives can drive you pretty crazy. In most cases, however, there's this commitment that family will be there for you even when nobody else will.

A truly rich man is one
whose children run into his arms
when his hands are empty.
—Author Unknown

We have an innate desire to belong, and family is usually the place for us to do that. As Christians, we belong to a larger family, one that goes far beyond our closest kin. It's a family that's headed by a loving Father, too—One who watches and waits for us, and welcomes us with open arms, no matter who we are or where we've been.

God calls us to be part of his family. In Ephesians 1:5, we're told that his "unchanging plan has always been to adopt us into his own family by bringing us to himself through Jesus Christ. And this gave him great pleasure."

Remember when you were a kid playing some sport, and it came down to picking teams? The best players were always picked first, weren't they? Some people didn't get picked at all. They were just the last ones, kind of like leftovers. What a feeling. You must know that there are people who have lived their entire lives like that, feeling like they're always the last ones picked.

But I have really good news. God's desire, above all, is to pick us. We've all been picked for God's team, and we're part of the first draft. He wants each of us to be part of his family through rebirth into his kingdom. And we're not just part of his family when we're in an actual church building or when we're attending a Bible study. We're his kids all day long, every day. We can be assured that he hasn't forgotten us.

Here on earth, we fathers do the best we can, but we're human and we sometimes mess up. God, on the other hand, doesn't mess up. As head of the church family, he doesn't make mistakes. He's perfect in everything he does. By default, then, God's a perfect father to us, as well.

called by name

So what does that mean? First, it means that God is a passionate father, One who's equally passionate about each of his kids. As he says in Isaiah 43:1, "Do not be afraid, for I have ransomed you. I have called you by name; you are mine."

Now, when God calls you by name, it's not like one of those salesmen who's been taught to learn the name of the person and call it. I don't know about you, but I get irritated by salesmen who don't know me but still pretend like they do because they know my name. Nobody calls me John. It's John Ed, and when someone calls me otherwise, I know that person's a phony. God, on the other hand, not only knows our names, he also knows us. That's important.

One year around Christmastime, a couple of boys went to a preacher and asked him if there was anything they could do for someone else in the spirit of the season. The preacher suggested they go read to a member of the church who was blind, and they agreed.

When the boys went to visit the man who was blind, they asked if they could read him something from the Bible. He said, "Yes. Read my favorite part of the Christmas story, Matthew, the first chapter." Usually, when we think of the Christmas story, we think of later verses in the chapter that specifically talk about the birth of Jesus. The man wanted the boys to start reading at the beginning.

Matthew 1 begins with the genealogy of Jesus, and it consists of one name after another. Abraham was the father of Isaac, and Isaac was the father of Jacob, and Jacob was the father of Judah, and so on, and so on. As the boys started coming across names they couldn't pronounce, one of them said, "We'll just skip over these names."

The man said, "No, don't skip over the names. They're the most important part. They might just be a list of names to you, but to God, they were important. He put every name in that book, and that means he put my name in that book, too."

God loves each of us as if there were only one of us.

—Author Unknown

If you're a parent, you know how much anguish can go into picking just the right name for your child. Names can be filled with meaning and promise, and every time you speak a child's name, you call forth who that child will become. Consider, for example, God changing Abram's name to Abraham in Genesis 17:5. Abraham literally means "father of

many," and God gave the name as a promise of the generations that were to come, even though the elderly Abram had
not yet fathered a son. Good parents are like that. They see
the potential in their children, and help draw it out.

hero and role model

God, as a good father, is not just passionate and encouraging. He's also patient and forgiving, no matter how many
times we mess up. He promises to be there for us, to answer
us when we call and to help us out of the problems we get
ourselves into. Isn't that what a parent is supposed to do?

> You don't choose your family.
> They are God's gift to you,
> as you are to them.
>
> **—Desmond Tutu**

Do you remember, as a little kid, bringing a broken toy to
your dad and expecting him to fix it? Do you remember as a
teen or young adult, calling him with a questions about your
car or lawn, and knowing he'd have the answer, or fix it?

So much of the way we are with our children has to do
with the way our parents treated us when we were kids. They
set an example for us to follow, just as we do for the next
generation.

I tell you what: God sets a great example for us to follow.
And that's all fathers can really hope for. One of my heroes
growing up was a football player named Maxie Baughn, who
was a linebacker for the Baltimore Colts. He played in a
championship game one time against the New York Giants,
and Baltimore received a penalty due to a mistake on the part
of the referees. Maxie Baughn was the defensive captain for
Baltimore, and he was so outraged at the call that—in front of

thousands of people on television—he pulled off his helmet and threw it down. He said it bounced thirty feet in the air. They lost the game.

A few days later, Maxie Baughn was at home playing football with his son, who was about six. Something happened, and the boy made a mistake. As soon as he did, he reached up and pulled off his helmet and said, "Watch here, Daddy. Here's what you did." Then he threw his helmet down and bounced it as high as he could.

Baughn later said that he was devastated when he saw that his son had seen him doing the same thing, and was emulating him. That made Maxie Baughn change his whole attitude on the football field. That was the moment he realized that little eyes watched everything he did. Kids—whether they'll admit it or not—want to grow up to be just like their parents. And what young boys and girls need to see is an example of what it means to follow after Jesus Christ.

unsurpassed love

There was this little boy named Ronnie, and he was an illegitimate child. He didn't know who his daddy was, and his mother just didn't want him. From the time she brought him home from the hospital, his cries would irritate her. One day, she became so irritated that she threw him against the wall, severely hurting him. The state authorities came and took Ronnie away from his mother, and he was placed in several different foster homes. No matter where he went, Ronnie never felt at peace.

When Ronnie started school, he learned that if he couldn't get attention by being good, he could get it by being bad. He started acting up and discovered that the worse he acted, the more attention he got. The cycle continued, and he didn't pass.

Ronnie was still in the sixth grade when he was fifteen. At that point, the only time the other kids included him was when they were in gym class or outside at recess, playing ball. Everybody wanted to be on Ronnie's team because he was twice as big as anyone else. Ronnie continued acting up.

One day, a teacher decided that she'd had enough of his antics. She looked at him and said, "I'm through with you." She took him to the principal's office, where she announced, "Don't let him come back to my class. I don't ever want to see this kid again."

Mr. Bagwell, the principal, did a strange thing. He looked at Ronnie and asked, "Do you know somebody cares for you?"

Ronnie, of course, said, "No."

The principal continued, "Ronnie, there's somebody that cares about you. I care about you. And I want to tell you about somebody else who cares about you even more than I do."

Now, that principal took a risk, especially since he was in a public school. But he reached into his desk, pulled out a Bible, and told that boy about Jesus. He told Ronnie how much God loved him.

Ronnie responded, "I want to be with him. I didn't know anybody cared for me like that." Ronnie received Christ and became a member of God's family.

It didn't take long for Ronnie's entire attitude to change. Within weeks, he was promoted to the seventh grade, then the eighth, and then the ninth. Before the end of the year, Ronnie had caught up with his class. He went on to become an honor student, earn an ROTC scholarship, and serve faithfully as an officer in the armed forces—all because he learned that somebody cared.

Ultimately, it doesn't matter what our past is, or what our current circumstances are, either. All we need to know is that God, our father, wants us. He's standing at the door, waiting expectantly for us to arrive.

dive in

- *How important is it to me that God knows my name?*
- *Has there ever been a time that I have walked away from home and felt like I couldn't go back?*
- *How does my relationship with my own father affect the way I see God as a heavenly one?*

We cannot destroy kindred:
Our chains stretch a little sometimes, but they never break.
—Marquise de Sévigné

brothers and sisters in Christ

One of the most beautiful things we're given here on earth is family. We can be so blessed by our parents, our spouse, our kids, our brothers, our sisters, our cousins, you name it. And it doesn't have to be family by birth, either. It's not uncommon for those without blood relatives to make their own families of friends.

I've got a great family, and I'm proud to be a Mathison. The truth is, however, as important as I consider my family, God's family is even more important to me. Surprised?

I'm not alone in this. Jesus felt the same way. In Matthew 12:47–50, Jesus was speaking to a crowd when someone said, "Your mother and your brothers are outside, and they want to speak to you." The response of Jesus is interesting. He says, "Who is my mother? Who are my brothers?" Then he points to his disciples and says, "These are my mother and brothers. Anyone who does the will of my Father in heaven is my brother and sister and mother!"

The church is God's family on earth. From Jesus' words, we can know that he's not ashamed to call us his sisters and brothers. He, too, wants us to be part of the family, and to enjoy all of the blessings and privileges that entails. Sure, there are privileges to being a part of God's family. We have a rich lineage, not to mention an incredible inheritance on the way.

family of believers

In order to be part of the family, we have to know and have faith in Jesus. We're told in John 1:12 that, "To all who believed him and accepted him, he gave the right to become children of God." We can't earn our way into God's family, and we can't buy our way into it, either. We can't even marry into it. No, the only way we can become part of God's family is through faith in Jesus. Once we accept him, that's when we truly become children of God.

Do you know what happens next? We begin to understand that God's family was created so he could share his love with us, and so we could share that love with other people. As it says in 1 John 4:16, "God is love, and all who live in love live in God, and God lives in them."

When we join God's family, a wonderful thing happens. We find belonging, companionship, and fellowship.

People don't like to be isolated. They don't like to be alone. Yet, there are some folks who say, "Well, the church isn't important. I can just worship God the way I want to wherever I am." Biblically speaking, that's not really possible. Romans 12:5 says: "Since we are all one body in Christ, we belong to each other, and each of us needs all the others."

I've already shared how the Body of Christ is like the human body, with all its unique parts. The hand does one thing, and the eyes and ears do others. But they don't function in isolation. What if the hand said to the rest of the body, "I don't need you. I'm going to go over there and stay in that chair?"

How would that hand live? Without the heart pumping blood to it, without the cooperation of the rest of the body, it would just shrivel up and die. God didn't create us to be isolated. He created us to be in community and in family, and even though each of us has different work to do, we're all connected.

Have you ever used a pile of charcoal to start a fire for a cookout? Let's say you light one piece of charcoal, but then you pick it up and put it off to the side, by itself. Before long, that piece of charcoal is going to go out, because it can't burn by itself. But if you put fifteen pieces of charcoal together and light them, they keep on burning because they feed each other. They help warm each other.

The Bible knows nothing of solitary religion.
—John Wesley

Individuals work the same way. It's like in the great musical *West Side Story*. The leader of the gang described belonging to a gang as being in a family, complete with all the benefits of that relationship. "You're home with your own; when company's expected, you're well protected."

Someone may say, "I'm going to be a Christian all by myself," but before long, that person will get out into the world and become a target for Satan.

Gang members don't go anywhere alone. By the same token, Christians can be shot down pretty quickly without our gang because we can't deal with Satan alone. When the devil tries to deal with a group, he's in trouble.

strength in numbers

Another thing that happens when we become members of God's family is that we grow and stay spiritually healthy. In the New Testament, the words "one another" and "each other" are used more than fifty times. What that tells me is that we're supposed to support each other and keep each other on track. We're called to relate to each other. To love, encourage, forgive, admonish, and care for each other.

At the same time, we help hold each other accountable. Now, this is an important concept. Hebrews 3:13 says, "You must warn each other every day, as long as it is called 'today,' so that none of you will be deceived by sin and hardened against God." Any of us is capable of committing any sin, and Satan knows this. It is unfortunate, but we can look back through history and see stories of people who were thought to be so strong in their faith, yet they fell to one temptation or another. When we stick together and hold each other accountable, we help keep each other out of trouble. Think of it this way: It's the banana that's away from the bunch that gets peeled.

Think about the mighty sequoia tree and its amazing size and strength. There's something else you should know about sequoias; they have very shallow root systems. They also have very *connected* root systems. They grow near other sequoias so they can intertwine their roots, brace each other, and hold each other up. Individually, they may fall, but collectively, they can stand for years and years and years.

multiply

We can't forget another thing that families do that extends to the church family, as well. We multiply. One of the most beautiful parts of being married is having children. In God's family, the way we do that is make disciples and bring other people under the umbrella of God's love.

It's important to note that God reiterates the idea that we're to reproduce as a command, not a suggestion. Matthew 28:19 says, "Go and make disciples of all the nations"; Mark 16:15 says, "Go into all the world and preach the Good News to everyone, everywhere"; Luke 24:47 says, "Take this message of repentance to all the nations"; and John 20:21 says, "As the

Father has sent me, so I send you." Sometimes we don't get the picture that these are commands. We just think of them as things to consider.

In college, students have some required classes to take for their majors and some classes that are electives. The electives are the ones students can choose. Telling other people about Christ is not an elective; it's a command. It's a command that's so important that it was the last one Jesus gave in the book of Matthew.

> ## A Christian that is not witnessing will soon have nothing to witness to.
>
> **—E. Stanley Jones**

So how do we add to God's family? We do it by focusing on one life at a time. If each one of us would introduce just one person to Jesus Christ and bring them into God's family, it's amazing what could happen. That person could bring one in, and the next person could bring one in, and so on.

We have to understand the difference between addition and multiplication. Let's suppose ten thousand individuals became Christians today alone. Then another ten thousand came to know Jesus every day this year. That sounds like a lot, but even if ten thousand people were converted every day for the next sixty-six years, that wouldn't even cover everybody in the United States.

Compare that to multiplication. Let's say you were the only person in the world who was a Christian today. Let's say over the course of the next year, you bring just one person to know Jesus. And the next year, both of you bring one person into the family. The year after that, each one of you brings somebody to know Jesus, and the number has jumped from one to two to four to eight. If you kept going like that, with each person bringing in another one every year, we could see the entire world come to know Christ in our time here on earth.

growing up and expanding

If, along the way, one of us breaks that chain, there's no telling how many people will be lost. Unfortunately, even when we become members of God's family ourselves, we may be unwilling to help expand it. One reason may be that we're still just immature in the faith. Babies, as you know, can't reproduce. They have to grow up and mature first, and Christians are the same way. We have to mature in order to understand the importance of our calling.

A man is called selfish
not for pursuing his own good,
but for neglecting his neighbor's.
—Richard Whately

Now, I don't mean that we have to have all our ducks in a row to start sharing the love of God with other people. Not at all. That's like waiting until all the traffic lights are green before we leave the house. If we do that, we'll never get anywhere. There is something to be said, however, for growing and maturing in the faith. We do that by reaching out to God and to the other members in our church family. We do that by interlocking our root systems with others, so we can all grow.

Immaturity isn't the only reason we sometimes neglect making more disciples. Sometimes, people can simply be unconcerned. Jonah is a great example of that. In 4:1–11, we learn that he argued with God over the city of Nineveh. He sat down on a hillside, and God caused a plant to grow up and cover him from the sun. Jonah, we're told in verse 6, was "very grateful for the plant." But the next day, God allowed a worm to eat the plant away, and between the hot sun and the scorching wind, Jonah became so miserable he wanted to die.

God's response? He said:

You feel sorry about the plant, though you did nothing to put it there. And a plant is only, at best, short lived. But Nineveh has more than 120,000 people living in spiritual darkness, not to mention all the animals. Shouldn't I feel sorry for such a great city?

When we look around us, it's easy to be thankful for those who are close, the ones we consider family. But once we understand what our place in the family of God really means, it's important for us remember that expanding that family is supposed to be our number one priority. There are so many men and women out there who are looking for brothers and sisters and a place to belong.

God has already loved them and called them his children; can't we open the doors and call them brothers and sisters?

dive in

- *Am I as willing to claim Jesus as my sibling as he is with me?*
- *In what ways can I interlock my root system with other members of the church family?*
- *Who could I help bring into God's family?*

No man is an island, entire of itself;
every man is a piece of the continent.

—*John Donne*

chapter 18

family gatherings

W hen you were a kid, did your family meet at the table for dinner every night? Was there an expectation that you'd be there, pulling up your chair with the rest of them? There was a time when that happened in pretty much every household. Dad would come home from work, Mom would have cooked, and the kids would come in from playing outside with friends just in time for everyone to sit down together.

My, how things have changed. Recent statistics say that fewer than one third of all kids sit down to eat dinner with both parents on any given night.

The unfortunate part is that when those meals went by the wayside, we lost more than just some good old-fashioned home cooking. We also lost a real time of connection. Family dinners were a time to hear about each other's days. They allowed real conversations without a television drowning out the words.

Granted, not everybody was lucky enough to sit down with a family that openly discussed issues or problems, and encouraged each other with kind words and great wisdom. For some, those family dinners might have been a time when the kids argued, Dad was distracted, and Mom seemed a little tired. Regardless of how it all played out, the important part was that everyone was there. Everyone could be counted on to be in their seats when they were supposed to be, and there was a certain comfort in the regularity and expectation of that. No matter what was going on outside, down the street or in the world, dinner was a time that families came together as one.

What happens without that connection? Everybody starts going his or her own way. In fact, a study by Columbia University found that teens who come from families that rarely eat dinner together are 72 percent more likely to use alcohol, illegal drugs, and cigarettes than the average teen. When we go off on our own, we lose that sense of strength in numbers—not to mention our sense of accountability. It's the lone sheep who wanders off that is most susceptible to the attack of the wolf.

In the same way, when we stop hanging around other Christians and start spending more time with people who have different priorities, our own priorities can start changing, too. If we don't spend time with others who focus on praying, attending worship services, serving God, and reading their Bibles, we may find that we do those things less and less, as well.

staying connected

We've talked about the church being God's family, and how much God wants us to be a part of it. So here's the thing: Just as with any family, we lose our sense of connectedness when we don't regularly come to the table. Coming together is what healthy families do; dysfunctional families, on the other hand, are fragmented. If we're going to be a healthy congregation, it's important that we take that sense of connectedness seriously. It's important that others can depend on us to be in our places, and that we can depend on others to do the same.

It helps to understand the power that's available when we're all present and pitching in. I'll give you an example. I heard about a man who was a farmer in Nebraska. Floodwater kept getting into his barn, so he decided it should be moved to higher ground. There was a place approximately 143 feet away where he could build a foundation, but he had no idea how to actually move the barn over there. His son, however, had an idea: "Let's get all of our friends and just pick it up and move it." His son then put steel tubing all around the barn with handles on it.

> No circumstances can make it necessary for a man to burst in sunder all the ties of humanity.
>
> **—John Wesley**

The farmer, knowing that the barn weighed about seventeen thousand pounds, was doubtful that the plan would work. But his son persisted. If they gathered enough people, he reasoned, the individual load wouldn't be that bad.

They rounded up 344 of their friends, and each one grabbed a handle. With that many people, each one was only responsible for about fifty pounds. Believe it or not, those 344 people all lifted at the same time, and moved that barn 143 feet in the span of three minutes. That's the kind of thing that happens when everybody's there, pitching in.

support system

It doesn't even have to be on that grand a scale. The writer of Ecclesiastes, for example, tells us in the fourth chapter that, "Two are better than one, because they have a good return for their work. If one falls down, his friend can help him up." When people are alone and they fall, that's bad news. They can be in real trouble.

I'll be honest and tell you that there are some places in my city that I won't go by myself. They're just scary. I'm not very strong, and I'm not very fast, so you're not ever going to see me there alone. We have some big guys in our church, professional football players. I'll tell you what: I'll go anywhere downtown with them, at any time of the day or night. They won't be afraid at all, so I won't either. There are some things I just can't do by myself, but when someone else is with me, it makes all the difference in the world. As it says in Ecclesiastes 4:12, "A person standing alone can be attacked and defeated, but two can stand back-to-back and conquer." And I'll let them do the defending for me.

Cooperation is the thorough conviction that nobody can get there unless everybody gets there.

—Virginia Burden

There are other ways we help each other, too. Sometimes I'll be on a mountaintop, and everything will be going just great. I'll be enthusiastic and full of faith and excited. At the same time, you may be walking through a valley of tough times, wondering how you're ever going to get out. Or the roles may be reversed. It's in those moments that we can reach out to each other in a significant way. When we're present, we can help pick each other up.

presence

Now, it's important to note that there's a difference between presence and attendance. You can be somewhere physically without actually being there emotionally, spiritually, or psychologically. I want to be clear that when I'm talking about the benefits of being present, I mean really being present—being plugged in and aware of the people and situations around us. It's only when we're really present that we can be of any use to someone else. When we're only in physical attendance, but not reaching out or not willing to listen, we may actually do more harm than good. Even if we're simply distracted, we may come across as uncaring or self-centered, instead.

It's amazing how many people come into a church simply looking for some level of comfort, or to find someone welcoming and kind. A lot of people don't get that in their everyday lives otherwise. So when they come into a church in which the members are not committed, present, and excited to be there, they may wonder why they're wasting their time.

It's even worse when people outside the church see members only half-committed to being at church on a regular basis. A man once told me about a neighbor who had been inviting him to church. On Sunday mornings, when he'd look over and still see his neighbor's car sitting in the driveway while the service was going on, his impression was that going to church must not be that important. "Evidently it didn't mean that much to him," he said. Ouch.

knowledge is power

Coming together isn't just about encouraging each other and helping lift each other up, though. It also gives us a chance to teach each other. When Paul wrote to the Colossians in 3:16, he said, "Let the word of Christ dwell in you richly as you teach and admonish one another with all wisdom." Similarly, when he wrote to the church at Ephesus, he said that it's their responsibility to "equip God's people to do his work and build up the church, the body of Christ" (4:12).

When we all learn that we have something to teach—and something to learn from others—that's when great things happen. We let go of pride and really walk in humility, understanding that none of us has all the answers—but together, we can come pretty close.

God didn't give any of us all of his wisdom, and there's no one on earth who's been through everything there is to go through. Our different personalities and unique experiences give us perspectives on situations that literally nobody else shares.

When we get together as a church family, then, we can teach each other, we can learn from each other, we can encourage each other, and we can help lift each other up. Note that not everything that happens is horizontal, or between people. Some of what happens when we come together is vertical, or between the people and God. Ultimately, when we come together as a congregation, we can worship God and celebrate his goodness together. And it doesn't always have to be in structured settings. Getting together for church parties, activities, or even potlucks can also draw people together.

The larger the island of knowledge, the longer the shoreline of wonder.
—Ralph W. Sockman

Think about the people closest to you, and I'll bet that one of the reasons that they're close is because you have a lot of shared experiences with them. Maybe you like the fact that they make you laugh. Maybe they've cried when you've cried, or shared your happiness when something has gone your way. Regardless, the time you've spent together has built a solid relationship, one that's probably quite different than it was the day you met.

quality time
We, as a church family, can grow in that same way. By spending quality time together, by coming together week after week, we can learn what's important to each other, so we know how to lift each other up in prayer. We can also learn each

other's stories. That way, if someone has a need that we personally don't know how to fill, we may know someone else who's been in a similar situation and could help close the gap.

A shared history is a beautiful thing. It opens a lot of doors, and it allows things like intimacy, trust, and transparency to come in. Really knowing each other develops more understanding and forgiving, and also creates an atmosphere in which people feel like they can be real. We can let our guards down and be more willing to confide in one another and share our burdens. That's when things get really good. That's when we become a healthy family, one that's not only willing to come to the table, but one that's excited to be there and interested in hearing about each other's days.

dive in

- *How have my own family experiences shaped the way I feel about the idea of the church as family?*
- *Do I feel compelled to meet with my church family regularly? Why or why not?*
- *What does my presence bring to the family table?*

chapter 19
where priorities lie

If you've ever sat and watched a football game in the rain, this one's for you. A lot of people really like football. They get a ticket, and they go. It doesn't matter if it's rainy or sunny, they go. It doesn't matter how many times they've been before or how long it's been since they last went. It doesn't even matter if the band is still playing the same songs that they played the last time they were in the stadium. It's a football game, so they're going to go. Period.

I recently came across a list of reasons that somebody wrote about why he won't go to football games anymore. Now, don't take it too seriously. Just keep in mind that the person who wrote it was also quite a churchman, so you might see some similarities. Here are the top ten reasons, he says, that he stopped heading for the stadium:

1. The band always plays songs I haven't heard before.
2. I can stay home and watch the game on television.

3. I played when I was in junior high, and I disagree with the way they coach now.
4. My parents made me go to football games when I was a child. I'm going to let my kids decide for themselves.
5. They're always asking you for money when you go to the stadium.
6. Sometimes you have to stay late because the game goes into overtime.
7. There might be someone at the game who's wearing the same thing I am.
8. I'm not going because it's too hot or too cold.
9. People at the game are unfriendly and don't speak to me when I go.
10. They keep changing things. They change the uniforms, the stadium, the plays, the coaches. I just don't like change, so I'm not going to go.

In the context of football, these excuses all come across as ridiculous, don't they? But in the context of going to church? Unfortunately, they're all too familiar. It can be easy to find an excuse. Someone's always asking for money. Nobody will speak to you. Things keep changing. And besides, can't you just stay home and watch a service on TV? You're not the first one to have thought it, and surely, you won't be the last.

In time of test, family is best.

—Burmese proverb

We've talked about the up sides of meeting together on a regular basis, all the good stuff. Attending worship services, remember, allows us to encourage each other, to lift each other up, teach each other, and praise God together. Now, though, we'll cover the down side. In other words, we'll look at the different reasons people give for not showing up.

outside looking in

I'd like to start, though, by telling you what the outside world sees. The people out there pay attention to how committed we are to this church thing, and how serious we are about making our relationship with God a priority.

I recently met a man named Ken, whose life was a total mess just five years ago. He had been an alcoholic and a compulsive gambler, but God transformed his life. Ken shared with me part of how that happened.

Every year, their firm would send Ken and another man to Florida for a weekend of golf. "We always looked forward to those three days of golf," Ken told me.

It didn't take Ken very long to notice something. "I realized that the first time we were down there on Saturday afternoon, he got in his car and drove back home. So I asked him, 'Where did you go? Is there trouble at home?'

He said no, so I asked him why he went home. And he told me, 'Tomorrow is Sunday, and I go to church on Sunday.' I said, 'You mean you'd give up a day of golf in Florida on the company to go home and go to worship?'

He replied, 'That's right. That's important to me.'"

His friend's commitment to attending church had a profound impact on Ken's life. He started thinking about how his friend really believed in something. It was through that example, Ken said, that his own life was turned around.

So what about you? Is your commitment to being at church so strong that other people would take note of it? If not, it might be time to figure out why.

busy, busy

One of the top reasons people give for not going to church is that they're just too busy.

The reality is that we live in a busy world. And everybody in the church is busy, too. Let's look at the story of Mary and

Martha to put things in perspective. It's found in Luke 10:38–42. Jesus was traveling with his disciples, and a woman named Martha opened her home to him. She had a sister named Mary, and when Jesus arrived, Mary planted herself at the feet of Jesus and hung on every word. Martha, on the other hand, was the more industrious of the two. Verse 40 tells us that she was worrying over the big dinner preparations. In the midst of all of her rushing around, she became frustrated with her sister, and said to Jesus, "Lord, doesn't it seem unfair to you that my sister just sits here while I do all the work? Tell her to come and help me."

But Jesus didn't tell Mary to help her sister. Instead, he rebuked Martha: "My dear Martha, you are so upset over all these details! There is really only one thing worth being concerned about. Mary has discovered it—and I won't take it away from her."

There's simply no excuse for being too busy. If you're too busy to study God's Word and to pray, then you're too busy. If you're too busy to come and worship together as God said to do, then you're too busy. And when you're that busy, there's no telling what you're missing out on.

> The best in man can flourish only when he loses himself in a community.
>
> **—Albert Einstein**

In Luke 14:16–24, there's a story that's often called the parable of the great banquet. Jesus is at the house of a leader, and he tells the tale of a man who was planning a big party. He invited a lot of people, and many said they would come. But when the day actually arrived and everything was ready, the invited guests began making excuses, saying they wouldn't be there. The host was angry, but what was he to do? He said to his servant, "Go quickly into the streets and alleys of the city and invite the poor, the crippled, the lame, and the blind." Beyond that, he urged the servant, "Go out into the country lanes and behind the hedges and urge anyone you find to come, so that the house will be full."

It's not such a stretch to see God as the host, inviting people to his banquet. But there's no way we can imagine the pain he felt when the people chose not to come. By the time he had extended the invitation to the unworthy—and that would be us—it had become an invitation of mercy. He was—and is—bound and determined to fill his table with anyone who will accept his gracious offer.

> They say that God is everywhere, and yet we always think of him as somewhat of a recluse.
>
> —Emily Dickinson

Yet, how often do we still make excuses? How often do we still refuse to come? How that rejection must still hurt God's heart!

I challenge you: The next time you think about not being at worship, ask yourself if it's just an excuse that's keeping you away. If it is, remember that the host who invited you is waiting—and you have no idea what might be on the table.

A member of our congregation told a story about an experience he had with making excuses that almost cost him a great deal. He was a busy man, but he said he'd go on a mission trip. The closer the time came for the trip, however, the more excuses he began to find not to go. He had excuse after excuse. Finally, he just got over it and decided to go anyway.

What happened? While he was on that trip, God called him into the ministry, and he also met his wife. What if he had given in to all the reasons he shouldn't go? How much would he have missed?

getting along

Some people won't attend worship because, some-where along the way, they got their feelings hurt. A man once told me:

> John Ed, wouldn't church be great if you didn't have any people? I mean, let's not have any people, and then we won't have any folks getting upset, and nobody would be hurting each other. Let me say to every person, you're going to get your feelings hurt. When you get around people, you're going to find folks who disagree with you and think differently and disappoint you. But church isn't about getting my feelings hurt. It's about following God and about making allowances for other people's faults. Church is about being forgiven and being forgiving—not about my feelings.

Wouldn't it be great if we could all get that? We've all been forgiven much by God, so doesn't it make sense that we would be willing to forgive much in other people? Let's believe the best about them, that they didn't hurt us on purpose, and move on with the task at hand.

meeting needs

There's a third excuse, and I've heard this one a lot. I've had folks tell me, "The church just isn't meeting my needs." I want you to pay close attention to this: The church doesn't exist to meet your needs. It doesn't exist to meet my needs. It exists to exalt Jesus Christ and to help us walk in his steps. Jesus didn't say to the Father, "Hey, my needs aren't being met." No, he laid down his life. And he called us to do the same.

This family we're part of is not here to meet our needs. It's not all about us. Look at what Paul says in Philippians 2:3–4:

> Don't be selfish; don't live to make a good impression on others. Be humble, thinking of others as better than yourself. Don't think only about your own affairs, but be interested in others, too, and what they are doing.

There's another part of that selfishness trap. It's the excuse of thinking we can be good Christians all by ourselves. If you ever find yourself believing that you don't need the church, I would urge you to read Romans 12. That's where we learn that we're all important members of the body.

Consider the fact that we can only find our meaning and function when we're part of a larger body. I personally don't think there's any way that a person can be a Christian totally by themselves. The whole nature of community and family is that we're in this together.

Consider the testimony of a man who told me, "You know, after we married and then had kids, we had to go to church. I told my wife, we need to go to church for the kids' sake. We want to raise our kids in the church. So that's why we came: for the kids. But when I got here, I discovered I was the one who needed it. It wasn't just the kids. It was me."

I think, collectively, something happens through a family that can never happen to an individual alone. But if we're not willing to show up—if we're so busy making excuses that we never even get our feet in the door—we miss out on more than we know.

dive in

- *What kind of excuses have I made for not attending church?*
- *How could my absence affect other members of the congregation?*
- *If people outside the church looked at my attendance record, what kind of conclusions would they be likely to make?*

*Every individual has a place to fill in the world and
is important in some respect whether he chooses to be so or not.*
—Nathanial Hawthorne

chapter 20

do your part

A number of years ago, our church teamed up with another church to help find a bone marrow match for a very sick little boy in our city. We raised money to offset the costs of people registering to become bone marrow donors, and also asked people from our congregations to consider registering themselves, in case there was a match. About two thousand people from our church ended up getting registered.

It was such a great effort, so I was going to give a little award to the people who had organized it all. That Wednesday night, just before I headed out the door, I received a phone call from a woman in our church who said, "John Ed, guess what? I'm so excited! I just received a call from the National Marrow Donor Program Registry and they found a match for me. I've got a chance to live! I want to thank the church because I found a match." She, too, had been sick, and had been waiting for just the right person to register.

I shared in her joy, and then proceeded to the Wednesday night dinner to present that plaque. I then took the opportunity to relay the good news the woman had told me. Suddenly, there was a shriek from a young lady in the back of the fellowship hall. She stood up and just started crying. Everybody got quiet.

Then she yelled, "I just got a phone call from the National Marrow Donor Program Registry and they told me they found a match for my marrow today!" It was those two who had matched. We had assumed it was somebody in Idaho or California or some other place in the world—but here they were, two people from the same church family. Isn't that a great story?

One of the things that's so great about it is that it's a real picture of how important every single individual is. It also shows that when we're willing to fully commit to being a part of the family and doing whatever the family needs done, there's no telling how deep those connections can go. There's no telling how far-reaching our efforts can become, even if they seem small or insignificant to us.

living witness

There was a famous preacher of another generation, and in the community where he lived, there was an intellectual agnostic. As the story goes, people had tried time and time again to get him to come to church, but to no avail. Finally, he agreed. He told a friend that he would go for two months, but still didn't believe it would do any good. So the preacher, knowing that the man was coming, decided to spend extra time preparing sermons that could address the faith for an intellectual agnostic. He worked and worked, and when the time came, articulately delivered his messages.

At the end of the two months, when the invitation was given, the intellectual agnostic stepped into the aisle, came forward and said he'd like to profess Christ as his savior and be baptized. It was a remarkable miracle.

The great preacher exclaimed his joy, and then asked a personal question for his own edification. He asked the new Christian which one of his sermons had been the turning point.

The man, however, admitted that none of the preacher's sermons did the trick. Instead, he told him that every week when he came to church, he noticed a woman who didn't have much money, didn't have much education, and had been through a lot. Nevertheless, her face glowed, and he wished he had the faith she did.

The previous week, he said, he had tripped on the way out the door of the church, and the woman had reached down and grabbed him by the elbow to pull him up. "When our eyes came face to face," he said, "she looked at me and simply said, 'Do you love Jesus like I love Jesus? And has Jesus changed you like he's changed me?' And I had to say no." The agnostic, then, became a Christian because of what the woman had said and done.

> Act as if what you do
> makes a difference. It does.
> —**William James**

The truth is, most people aren't converted by sermons or Sunday school lessons. Those things help. But most people come into the faith because somebody else simply looks them in the eye and shows them a changed life. That's the kind of credibility that makes the difference.

team player

Because we all come from different backgrounds and have different stories and experiences, we relate to people in different ways. There are people who will connect with you in ways they can't with me, and vice versa. All together, we can form a wide net that catches the lonely, the hurting, and the lost. And that's a whole lot more effective than each one of us just running around with our individual fishing poles. For that to happen, though, we've got to recognize the things in each of us that make us unique. We've got to know where we fit in, as well as the places someone else can help pick up where we leave off.

I was recently with one of the greatest coaches in America, Grant Teaff. He's now the executive director for the American Football Coaches Association, a position he's held for more than a decade. He coached a national championship team and had two All-Americans. One of them was a 285-pound offensive lineman, and the other was a 160-pound wideout, someone whose primary job was to catch passes from the quarterback. That wideout was fast as lightning.

Teaff said, "Wouldn't I have been foolish as a coach to tell this 160-pound wideout, if you're an All-American, let's see you come in here and play offensive tackle? Man, they'd run him over. Or if I'd said to that 285-pound offensive tackle, hey, you get out here at wideout. If you're an All-American, let's see you operate. They can't play another position. But they're All-Americans at their positions."

Indifference is the essence of inhumanity.
—George Bernard Shaw

We all have our positions, too. We can't just go all over the place trying to play somebody else's position; we've got to play our own. When I play my position and you play yours—and we do it to the best of our ability, supporting and encouraging each other—that's when our team really starts to win. That's when our family really starts to expand. But for us to get organized, for us to really pull it off, we've all got to be there. It goes back to making a commitment to be present. We've all got to show up.

Unfortunately, we don't do so well at coming to church. We live in a football-crazy society, and Sunday's a big game day.

Now, I realize this is a dangerous statement that I'm going to make, but let me tell you: There are some things that are more important than football. Coming together in church is one of them. The most important victories are not won in a stadium; they're won in the hearts and lives of people.

I read a story about a man named Giles Pellerin, who was a big fan of the University of Southern California. He was actually known as USC's super fan because he attended 797 consecutive USC football games. Since 1926, he never missed a game, and it's estimated that he traveled more than 650,000 miles and spent more than $85,000 maintaining his run. Pellerin died in 1998 at the age of ninety-one, and do you know where he was when it happened? At the UCLA-USC ball game. He died doing what he loved to do best.

authentic fellowship

What if Christian folks could get that excited? What if we worked on attending services with that kind of dedication? If we did, we could find fellowship the way it's supposed be. Fellowship is about trust and intimacy. It's about crying with each other, laughing with each other, and sharing with each other. It's about being honest and reliable and trustworthy. It's being someone who can hear or say, "Hey, here's what I'm struggling with and I really need your help."

All too often, though, without commitment, churches become places where people just put their best foot forward. People come in and try to look like everything's just rosy. We wear masks and façades. In some congregations, we can sit next to the same family Sunday after Sunday and never know their name. But when we're willing to risk who we are, get to know others, and trust that people are going to accept us regardless, that's when we can be human.

We all make mistakes, and as such, our first response to each other ought to be mercy. As we're taught in Colossians 3:13,

"You must make allowance for each other's faults and forgive the person who offends you. Remember, the Lord forgave you, so you must forgive others."

Such fellowship reflects God's grace and mercy. He has compassion for us, and in true fellowship, we have compassion for others. We forgive. We don't judge. We don't gossip. we trust that others will treat us as they want to be treated. We should be a church family that quickly forgives each other, so when people on the outside are looking in, they know that they can come in and be forgiven, too, no matter who they are or what they've done. God's family should be one that celebrates the uniqueness of each individual, but at the same time, is a picture of unity.

I've noticed something over the years. I've learned that when you talk to people who are really involved in their church, they always use the pronoun "we." Ask them about their church, and it's "we" this, and "we" that. But if you talk to someone who attends but isn't really committed, you'll hear a lot of "they."

People who work together will win,
whether it be against complex football defenses
or the problems of modern society.
—**Vince Lombardi**

It's all about ownership, not just of the body but also of the parts we play in it. It works the same way for football teams. Let's say a certain team isn't doing so well. If you ask some fans about it, they'll say, "Well, they're not playing so well right now." But other fans—the real ones—will say, "We aren't doing so well." Win or lose, they're still committed.

Ultimately, being willing to commit like that, devoting ourselves as individuals to the greater good, is all about love. The bottom line is that we love. Paul puts it beautifully in 1 Corinthians 13:1–3:

If I could speak in any language in heaven or on earth but didn't love others, I would only be making meaningless noise like a loud gong or a clanging cymbal. If I had the gift of prophecy, and if I knew all the mysteries of the future and knew everything about everything, but didn't love others, what good would I be? And if I had the gift of faith so that I could speak to a mountain and make it move, without love I would be no good to anybody. If I gave everything I have to the poor and even sacrificed my body, I could boast about it; but if I didn't love others, I would be of no value whatsoever.

May we, then, find our value through truly loving one another.

dive in

- *When I talk about my church, do I use the term "we" or "they"?*
- *Do I know my part in the family of God? If so, how willing am I to play it?*
- *How could I experience more genuine fellowship in my life?*

Remember upon the conduct of each
depends the fate of all.

—Alexander the Great

chapter 21

commit to community

Imagine a puzzle with its pieces spread across a table. Since we've been talking about presence, you probably know where this is going. It takes every piece of that puzzle in its correct place to create the overall picture. Each of us is needed to help our individual church body complete its picture, and our church body is needed to fulfill its role in the overall Body of Christ.

Now imagine one puzzle piece. It's unique. There is no other one shaped exactly like it. Of course, some look like it from afar. But when you try to place an individual piece, you see where it fits and where it doesn't.

That puzzle piece links with every piece that surrounds it. It may touch a half dozen other pieces all together. If it's not there, the pieces it's supposed to touch can't fully realize their roles either. It's not just that the overall picture isn't clear; it's that it's fuzziest in the place where the piece is missing.

Could it be the same way with our church body? The overall picture isn't clear when we're not there, but could there be those more directly affected by our absence? Are there those who we're supposed to touch or team up with who go unfulfilled when we aren't in our place?

pulling together

So often we think about going to church because we need it, or because we want to be fed. Those are, admittedly, crucial parts of the church experience. But what about what we put into it? We're there to worship God, and we should put our hearts fully into that. We also need to fully pour ourselves into touching our brothers and sisters while we're at it. It may be as simple as a warm smile at a visitor, or holding open the door for a young mother juggling a baby and a diaper bag. It may be praying for someone, offering an encouraging word, or filling in as usher or nursery worker when there's a shortage.

Presence is about being where we're expected, but it's also about being present while we're there. Are we distracted by our thoughts or daydreaming about who's winning the game? Are we worried about the pot roast burning while the service goes on? Are we sitting through a small group meeting constantly checking our cell phone for messages? Or are we fully present in that moment, attentive to hear from God, but also to serve the needs of our brothers and sisters?

When I don't show up, who do I let down? How can I be more present and fully engaged?

God our father

Perhaps you've heard the saying, "God doesn't have any grandchildren." See, just because your parent was a Christian, it doesn't mean you're automatically one, too. Just because your name has been on the roll of that church since you were born doesn't make you a child of God either. God wants a relationship with each of us, a personal and genuine relationship that doesn't rely on how we were raised.

Of course, there are many, many benefits that go along with being a child of God. First, we have a Father—a Daddy, if you will—who created the universe, who is all powerful. And what an inheritance we have! It is God's "good pleasure to give you the kingdom," as Jesus said in Luke 12:32 (NKJV).

Now, if we discovered we were in line for the throne of some country, who wouldn't show up to accept the crown, the palace, and all that went with it? Wouldn't we crow to everyone around, appear on a few TV shows, and allow newspapers to document our ascension to the throne?

Then why do we ignore our spiritual inheritance? Why do we act like paupers when we're really princes?

It must have been extremely difficult for the prodigal son to return home in the first place. How long do you think it really took him, though, to get out of servant mentality and accept his rightful place alongside his father? We can hope that he was grateful for his father's mercy, and that he showed his father appreciation every day. Did he refuse to move back into the family house and insist on living with the servants? I doubt it. As soon as his father put his ring on his finger, the son was back in the family.

What's preventing me from moving out of servant quarters and into the family home? In what ways am I still acting like a pauper?

brothers and sisters in Christ

If one of our responsibilities as a member of God's family is to reproduce, to keep the family name going, have you ever been directly responsible for someone coming to know the Lord? Have you ever shared your faith with someone?

If not, you may be spiritually barren, at least in this season in your life. Just as conceiving a child in the natural requires some action on your part, helping to bring forth spiritual life requires some action, too. You see, we can't merely sit by and hope and pray that someone we love comes to know the Lord. We have to be willing to share the good news—that's what "gospel" means, after all—with them. Sometimes we walk around so afraid that we might offend someone that we prevent even the tiniest seed from being shared.

Even if you grew up in the church, someone somewhere shared Jesus with you before you ever came to know him. Perhaps it was a Sunday school teacher or maybe a traveling evangelist. If you weren't reared in the church, how did you come to know God unless someone ventured out in faith and shared with you?

We need to do it. And if you get rejected, so what? Statistics show us that the average nonbeliever hears the gospel message almost seven times before he or she is willing to believe. Messages one through six are rejected, or so they think; but they're every bit as important as message seven.

Am I willing to risk rejection to help God's family grow?

family gatherings

Keep in mind that there is no perfect church, and there are no perfect church people. I've often heard it said that if you find a perfect church, you shouldn't join it. You'll only mess it up. Despite imperfections, though, there are many lessons our fellow church members can teach us. Are we willing to let them? Proverbs 27:17 tells us that we are like iron sharpening iron in each other's lives. Let me put it another way. The only way to get better at any sport is to consistently play with people who are better than you. It improves your game. If you consistently play people who aren't as good as you are, your game will be weakened.

Are you willing to be iron in someone's life, and to allow someone to be iron in yours? Every single person in our lives can be used to push us closer to God or to pull us away.

Who is influencing me? Are those influences pushing me closer to God, or drawing me away?

where priorities lie

You know, there's just no nice way to say it.

There are people in our church who can be annoying. They're always complaining or asking for help. They always require a little extra grace. Maybe they prevent you from wanting to come together as a family.

They may be the equivalent of that crazy aunt everyone tolerates at the holiday table. No one really wants to be stuck sitting next to her, hearing her stories again and again, having her criticize everything from the table decorations to everyone's appearance. While everyone complains about her behind her back, no one fully reaches out to her in love. They're polite, of course, but never genuine.

Don't make the mistake of thinking she doesn't notice that she's on the outside of the family's inner circle; that she's merely tolerated once a year. What a lonely place to be. She knows that no one would miss her if she weren't there. She knows that they might actually have a better time if she weren't. But she has nowhere else to go.

There are people like that in our church family. They don't really fit in, they tap dance on our last nerve, and they always seem to test the bounds of grace. But if they don't find a place in the family of God, where will they find a place? God accepts them for who they are and even created them with some of those unique characteristics.

Who will be there for us when we're a little needy or extremely annoying?

Am I willing to allow God to show me his heart for other people? Am I willing to accept them as he created them, or to allow him to determine what to change and when?

do your part

Take a look at a brick building. From a distance, each individual brick is pretty indistinguishable. You may be able to pick out a slightly different color here or there, but as far as being able to tell each brick's contribution? Not likely.

Now consider this: No matter how many bricks are in that building's façade, if only one was missing, the building would be weakened. Cold air would get inside. The brick above, the one relying on the missing brick for support, would be weakened. Eventually, that missing brick would have an impact on the whole building.

It's the same way with the church. We may be known collectively as a congregation, but within that, each person has an important part to play. We're all supporting bricks, linking with other bricks to help keep the cold out.

There's an old saying that 20 percent of the people do 80 percent of the work in any group situation. That's not how it should be in the church, but sadly, it is in many cases. In a lot of churches, it's easy to see that the people in the 20 percent are crucial to the life of the body. Without them, some things simply wouldn't get done. But what about the other 80 percent? Are they equally as important? You bet. No matter how involved a person is, he or she is just as important as everyone else. Each person has a part to play, no matter how big or small.

Am I playing my part? Have I ever judged someone who appears to be doing less than I am? Am I willing to accept my family members as important to the work of the church?

part IV

pennies in the
fountain

It is every man's obligation to put back into the world
at least the equivalent of what he takes out of it.
—*Albert Einstein*

chapter 22
maintaining balance

J ust in case you weren't paying attention in eighth-grade science class, let's go over the concept of the water cycle. It's also known as the hydrologic cycle, and it's the process through which rain travels from the sky to the earth and back again.

First—assuming there is a first in the cycle—water falls from the clouds to the ground in the form of rain, snow, or even hail. That's precipitation. Next, the moisture gathers in lakes, rivers, oceans, or other bodies of water, or it soaks into the soil and becomes ground water. That's known as collection. Evaporation is next, and that's when the water absorbs back into the atmosphere. Finally, there's condensation, in which the rising water cools, condenses, and turns into clouds. We all know what happens after that: The clouds release the rain, and the cycle continues.

If you think we've gotten completely off the topic, here's something to think about. That water cycle, which is as old as the earth, is a lot like another time-tested concept: the cycle of giving. By giving to God financially, we help the sequence of blessings continue.

Let's start with precipitation. In our science example, it's all about rain. In our giving example, however, it's all about the cash. Sometimes it's a drizzle and sometimes it's a downpour, but as Henry Wadsworth Longfellow said, "Into each life some rain must fall." So money comes into our lives through work, through gifts from other people, you name it. Sooner or later, money appears. We begin to collect it. Sometimes we collect it in the bank, and sometimes we collect it through the stuff we accumulate: cars, houses, whatever.

Now, when water collects and keeps on collecting without going anywhere, that water tends to get stagnant. Mosquitoes, bacteria, and parasites flourish in stagnant places, but a lot of other things die. In other words, hanging around in that water is not a very good idea. It's actually an unhealthy place to be, as it's a breeding ground for disease.

store treasures in heaven

Hanging around a pool of money that's not going anywhere can be the same thing. It can attract all sorts of problems. So much so that the Bible teaches against it. As Matthew 6:19 warns, "Don't store up treasures here on earth, where they can be eaten by moths and get rusty, and where thieves break in and steal." Instead, the next verse says, we're to store up our treasures in heaven, "where they will never become moth-eaten or rusty and where they will be safe from thieves."

Fair enough. But do you know how we're supposed to do that? That's where the evaporation part comes in. Now, before you think negative thoughts, I understand the feeling that money has just evaporated right out of your hand. That's not what I mean.

In order for rain to evaporate or go back up into the atmosphere, it has to be warmed by the sun. In order for our money to get back to the heavens so God can pour it out where he sees fit, we often have to be touched by a different kind of son, Jesus. He compels us to give whatever we have.

> When I have money, I get rid of it quickly, lest it find a way into my heart.
>
> —John Wesley

When we're motivated out of love, then, and give to the church through tithes and offerings, God gathers it up for his own purposes. And down here on earth, our once-stagnant pools begin to flow with life, replenishing themselves along the way. What goes up, it's often said, must come down. The more we allow our money to rise to the heavens, the more likely we are to see abundant rain.

A lot of people just don't get this concept. Maybe they slept through science class, or maybe nobody ever told them. An unfortunate thing tends to happen when it comes to money and the church. Preachers get uncomfortable with the subject because they're afraid to offend their congregations. They're afraid that they'll come across as takers with their hands out all the time, and that people won't want to give.

I don't have that fear. I know I have a responsibility to teach about the importance of giving back to God what's already his anyway, and to help the people around me be free and blessed. I'm not doing my congregation any favors by not telling them important biblical truth—no matter how candid it may seem.

give it back

Look at Malachi. He was a prophet in Jerusalem, and his job was to remind the Jews of their willful disobedience. He spoke the words of God, calling the nation to come back to him. And in 3:8, he said, "Should people cheat God? Yet, you have cheated me!" He explained:

> You have cheated me of the tithes and offerings due to me. You are under a curse, for your whole nation has been cheating me. Bring all the tithes into the storehouse so there will be enough food in my Temple. If you do . . . I will open the windows of heaven for you. I will pour out a blessing so great you won't have enough room to take it in! Try it! Let me prove it to you! Your crops will be abundant, for I will guard them from insects and disease. Your grapes will not shrivel before they are ripe . . . Then all nations will call you blessed, for your land will be such a delight.

It's one thing to think you might miss a blessing by not giving to God. It's another to understand that you're actually stealing from him. Look at the promise for those who will give: He'll pour out a blessing so great that we won't have room to take it in!

Of course, that shouldn't be our sole motivation for giving, but because God loves us, he wants us to be taken care of well. When we give generously, we show that we really do regard God and his commands seriously. "The purpose of tithing," we're told in Deuteronomy 14:23, "is to teach you always to fear the LORD your God."

Before we go any further, I want to make sure you understand what the word *tithe* means. A tithe is 10 percent of your income. Tithing is a controversial topic in some circles, but it pleases God. The purpose of giving it is to teach us to honor and revere God, to show that he's more important to us than anything we hold in our hands.

Now, when we talk about giving, there are different kinds. There's giving to the church, and there's also giving to those in need. Giving allows us to follow the selfless example Jesus set for us. It allows us to express our gratitude to God for the things he's already done.

stewardship

In Psalms 116:12, the psalmist asks, "What can I offer the LORD for all he has done for me?" And in Deuteronomy 16:17, we find our answer: "All must give as they are able, according to the blessings given to them by the LORD your God." In order to do that, we must be good stewards of what we have. To be a good steward means to use wisdom and discernment, rather than be foolish and haphazard, in our spending.

Jesus gives an example of stewardship in Matthew 25:14–30. A man was going on a trip. Before he left, he called together his three servants and gave them money to invest for him while he was gone. According to the story, he gave five bags of gold to one, two bags of gold to another, and one bag of gold to the last, "dividing it in proportion to their abilities."

> **Money is like manure; it's not worth a thing unless it's spread around encouraging young things to grow.**
>
> **—Thornton Wilder**

The servant who received the five bags of gold went to work right away. He took that money and invested it. Before long, his sum had doubled. The one who was given the two bags also doubled his money. But the one who received only one bag "dug a hole in the ground and hid the master's money for safekeeping."

Finally, the master returned. He called for his servants, and then asked them to give an account of what they had been given. Obviously, he was pleased with the work of the first two. Because they had been faithful in handling the small amounts, he announced that he would give them more responsibilities.

The third servant, however, the one who hid the money in fear of losing it, endured the wrath of his master. At the very least, the master said, he should have put the money in the bank where it could earn interest. He took the money back from the servant, and gave it to the one who already had ten. Jesus said:

> To those who use well what they are given, even more will be given, and they will have an abundance. But from those who are unfaithful, even what little they have will be taken away.

That third servant's downfall was self-centeredness. Because he was scared, he tried to protect himself by not letting anything happen to his master's money. As a result, he wasn't willing to take a risk. The other two, however, took great risks. We all know that investments don't always pay off.

I find it interesting that when the master originally handed the money to his servants, he wasn't really giving it to them. Rather, he was just entrusting it. The servants weren't told, "Do whatever you want with it, and if you make any extra, you can keep it for yourself." No, they were given the money to invest for the master. Two of the servants, because they put their master's potential gain first, ended up with more in the long run.

A man wrapped up in himself makes a very small bundle.

—Benjamin Franklin

It's the same with us, when God is our master. When he entrusts money to us—rains it down on us from heaven (big or small amounts, windfalls or what we earn at work)—we have the chance to make a difference on his account, regardless of our own.

When we fear the master so much that we hide what we wouldn't have except for him, we risk it evaporating out of our hands—and not in a good way. We risk falling prey to greed, self-centeredness, and pride.

Releasing money back into God's atmosphere is a chance for us to honor our master and to continue that cycle of blessings in our life. If we're willing to take part, we just might be as blessed as those servants in the story when their own master returned. Here's what he said: "Well done, my good and faithful servant . . . let's celebrate together."

Obviously, those risks paid off in ways better than those servants could have imagined. It can be the same for us.

dive in

- *How do I feel when the offering plate is passed at church? Do I dread it, or do I look forward to being able to give expectantly?*
- *How do I invest the bags of gold God has given me?*
- *How do I feel about the idea that I cheat God if I don't regularly give?*

*Find out how much God has given you and take from it
what you need; the remainder is needed by others.*
—St. Augustine

chapter 23
heavenly treasure

When you think about the teachings of Jesus, a lot of things probably come to mind: sacrifice, love, humility, and prayer may be your first thoughts. But there's one subject he spoke about more than any other. Would you be surprised to hear that it's money?

He had a lot to say on the topic. He believed, as he said in Matthew 6:21, "Wherever your treasure is, there your heart and thoughts will also be," and as such, wanted to make sure his followers had their priorities in order.

Judas didn't do so well. It was money, after all—thirty silver coins, to be exact—that motivated him to betray Jesus. He asked the leading priests, "How much will you pay me?" and the deed was done. Throughout the Gospels, we're warned against putting too much importance on it, we're taught to use it wisely, and we're shown that happiness doesn't come through cash.

Of course, those lessons run counter to the world's ideas of success and the emphasis placed on storing up wealth and possessions. Jesus even said in Matthew 19:23–24 that, "It is very hard for a rich person to get into the kingdom of heaven." He said that it is "easier for a camel to go through the eye of a needle than for a rich person to enter the kingdom of God!"

we cannot serve two masters

God doesn't frown on success; quite the contrary. Luke 12:32 tells us that it gives God "great pleasure" to give us his kingdom. What we need to be cautious of is that the more we have, the more prone we are to keeping our eyes on that treasure rather than keeping our eyes on God.

In Matthew 19:16–22, Jesus told the story of a rich young man who came to him and asked what good things he must do to have eternal life. In response, Jesus said he could receive eternal life if he kept the commandments. The young man asked which ones, and he ran down a list that included do not murder, do not commit adultery, and honor your father and mother, among other rules.

The young man said, "I've obeyed all these commandments. What else must I do?"

Jesus responded in verse 21: "If you want to be perfect, go and sell all you have and give the money to the poor, and you will have treasure in heaven. Then come, follow me."

> The best way for a person to have happy thoughts is to count his blessings and not his cash.
>
> **—Author Unknown**

Sad to say, the young man couldn't do it. It was just too much.

Now, when I read this story, I don't believe the lesson is that we should all give away everything we own. That's not what Jesus was teaching. Instead, I think Jesus was simply going straight to the heart of the matter. He knew that the young man put too much emphasis on his belongings, and wouldn't be able to give them up even if God asked him to. And I think a lot of us, in the same situation, wouldn't be able to give up everything either.

financial support

God understands that the way we view money is a window into our overall principles. He knows that we put money toward the things we value, but not to the things we don't. You know that old phrase, "Put your money where your mouth is." That sums it up: It's one thing to say something. It's another to give up your cash to support it.

So if we had to be honest, what are the things we truly value? Where does our money go? Are we willing to spend money the way that Jesus would have us spend it? If so, according to Matthew 10:8, we're told to "give as freely as you have received."

That money we hold to so tightly can be a tool that God can use to extend his Kingdom. It can buy Bibles, so people can read the Word of God. It can send missionaries, so people can hear the gospel. Or it can support a pastor, so he and his family can give their all to their congregation.

Now, I realize that not all Christian organizations have been perfect in handling their money. Christian organizations are made up of human beings, and human beings make mistakes. Regardless, there's a biblical principle about giving to support the works of the church, and it's found in Numbers 35:2–3. That's where God told Moses how to take care of the Levites, or the ministers, who were responsible for looking after the tabernacle. They had no worldly possessions of their own, so God ordered the people to give them land to live on, homes, and flocks. That way, they wouldn't have to spend their time worrying about where the next meal was coming from; they could totally commit their thoughts and actions to serving God. In the same way, we're called to support the church with our finances so it can do what it sets out to do as well.

money can't buy heaven

Now, there's something I want to be clear about. Giving money is not about giving enough to make yourself right with God. Some folks think that if they just give enough, they'll buy their way into God's heart, into heaven, into whatever. There are even some historic precedents where that was part of formal church law.

That's not how it works. Even if you gave every single penny you had, it still wouldn't give you faith in Christ. Giving is not a means of working our way into a relationship with God. Instead, it's a response to what God has already done for us. "Give as freely as you have received," remember?

Bread for myself is a material question.
Bread for my neighbor is a spiritual one.

—Jacques Maritain

Giving is also not a plan to become independently wealthy. I've heard some people say, "Well, God said if you give, he's going to bless you. So the best way to get rich is to give money so you can get it back." God does indeed say he's going to bless us. He also promises to take care of our needs. But when he blesses us in return for our giving, that blessing may not come in financial form. There may be other places we need it more. So if my motivation in giving is that I'm going to get more back, I'm missing the whole point.

a chance to be like Christ

Finally, the idea of giving is not some kind of church financial plan. The church didn't sit back and say, "You know, we've really got to raise some money, so let's ask all the people to give." As we've seen in the book of Numbers, it's an idea God instituted himself.

Giving actually provides a chance to be more like Jesus. I want you to hear me carefully on this: Becoming like Jesus isn't something that anybody can do on his or her own. God has provided a way through the Holy Spirit to live in us, and it's the Holy Spirit's job to help us become more like Jesus. Here's what Philippians 2:13 has to say about it: "For God is working in you, giving you the desire to obey him and the power to do what pleases him."

As we "let go and let God"—as our friends in twelve-step programs say—then, we find that our desire to be generous with others grows. When God is at work in us, and we really let him do his thing, he brings forth love, joy, peace, patience, kindness, goodness, faithfulness, gentleness, and self-control. We start to find that things that were once important to us really aren't that important any more.

Now, I don't believe that means Christians can't have nice things. We just won't have the same motivation behind them. We don't want the biggest house on the block, for example, just so we can impress the neighbors. We might find, somewhere down the line, that the reason we really want more income is so we can give more of it to other people.

While God is working all that other stuff within us, he's bound to increase our love for others at the same time.

In Acts 2:42, we're given a beautiful picture of the early church. We're told that, "They joined with the other believers and devoted themselves to the apostles' teaching and fellowship, sharing in the Lord's Supper and in prayer." Beyond that, though, they met together "constantly," and "shared everything they had." It says in verse 45:

> They sold their possessions and shared the proceeds with those in need. They worshiped together at the Temple each day, met in homes for the Lord's Supper, and shared their meals with great joy and generosity—all the while praising God and enjoying the goodwill of all the people.

Obviously, God was at work, because people aren't that generous by nature. There was an understanding that the brothers and sisters in Christ would help meet each others' needs, and that no one would want for anything. This powerfully illustrates the Golden Rule found in Matthew 7:12: "Do for others what you would like them to do for you."

Think of giving not as a duty but as a privilege.
—John D. Rockefeller Jr.

Continue on to the end of verse 47, and you'll see the end result: "Each day the Lord added to their group those who were being saved."

I'll bet one of the reasons so many people came into the church was that they saw that sense of commitment and community being played out. They saw that Christians were different from everybody else, and that they weren't afraid to either be vulnerable enough to express their own needs or to be generous enough to meet someone else's.

When we give—especially when we do so without expecting anything in return—that catches the world's attention. So many people want so many things from us. Everybody has an angle. But an angle of generosity is straight from God's heart.

witness of faith

Giving, then, represents an essential part of the Christian walk. It gives us a chance to show that God is actually real. It's an area in which he asks us to test him, and to trust him.

Consider Proverbs 3:9–10, which says:

> Honor the LORD with your wealth and with the best part of everything your land produces. Then he will fill your barns with grain, and your vats will overflow with the finest wine.

It's an if/then principle that requires us to step out in faith so he can meet us where we are.

use good judgment

Now, we need to be careful. We should make a habit of asking God where, when, and how much we should give. Some people try to take advantage of a generous heart.

I heard a sad, sad story about a TV preacher who said that if you needed healing, you could send him your name and address—and some money along with it—and he'd pray for you.

A lady took him up on that, and sent in her husband's name because he had cancer. That preacher wrote back and told her husband that he was praying for him. But you know what happened? That woman's husband died, but the preacher kept sending letters addressed to the husband, saying things like, "I woke up this morning and God told me to pray for you." The whole thing ended up in a lawsuit.

So remember, God calls us to be wise with our money. Even in giving, he doesn't expect us to generous to the point of being foolish. But when we look to the example God set for us—the fact that he literally gave everything when he sent his son to die for us—the least we can do is to part with a temporal thing like money when he asks.

dive in

- *How willing am I to meet other people's needs with my own money?*
- *How is God at work in me when it comes to money?*
- *Have I ever felt that I could buy myself into God's grace?*

You can never get enough of what you don't need
to make you happy.

—Eric Hoffer

chapter 24
keeping priorities
in line

When you're a preacher, you see and hear all kinds of stuff. Sometimes it's good. Sometimes I get to rejoice with people over the great things God has done. But sometimes, what I hear absolutely breaks my heart.

One of the saddest things that has ever occurred in my ministry happened about a decade ago. There was a family with several kids, and the father was an incredibly talented man—everything he touched turned to gold. He got raise after raise after raise, and they moved out of one house and into another, and out of that house and into another, and they ended up in a big house by the lake. Along the way, he found less and less time for family devotions. Then he gave up coming to Sunday night worship. He just didn't have the time.

From the outside, the family looked like a total success; but on the inside, it was falling apart. One of their teenage daughters came to visit me one day, and I'll never forget it.

She was crying and here's what she said: "You know what's happened to my family? We used to pray together as a family. We used to love each other. We used to come to church together. Now we don't. Daddy doesn't have time." She said, "John Ed, I want you to pray for something unusual. I want you to pray that my daddy will lose his job and we have to go back to the way things used to be."

I wish I could tell you that the story had a happy ending, but it doesn't. That girl's father did end up losing his job, but it was due to the fact that he had become an alcoholic. He was so driven by the pursuit of money, that he drove his family away and ended up losing everything he had.

Money can't buy me love.

—John Lennon and Paul McCartney

See, when we hold so tightly to money that it becomes the most important thing in our lives, everything else gets out of whack. Matthew 6:33 instructs us to make the Kingdom of God our primary concern, and when anything else takes first place, it becomes an idol. And we know how God feels about us having idols. They're listed in the "thou shalt nots" of the Ten Commandments.

return to sender

One of the ways to loosen our grip on money is to give it back to God. Giving reminds us that God has given us everything we have anyway.

I used to do little object lessons with the children on Sunday nights. One evening, I asked the kids to borrow something from somebody next to them and to come forward with it. There was a man who had just given his wife a beautiful anniversary ring, and their daughter borrowed the ring. She brought it down front.

One father had one of those fancy two-hundred-dollar fountain pens. His son said, "Dad, let me use it." At first the father said no, but then the boy said, "John Ed will give it back." So he brought the pen down front.

When I had finished my little lesson, I said a prayer and then told the kids to go back to their seats. I just stuck the pen and the ring in my pocket.

That little boy and girl just stayed there, looking at me. I said, "We're through. You can go on back."

But the girl said, "Hey, you've got our ring." I replied, "Oh, I'm just going to borrow it for a little while."

She asked, "How long?" I answered, "Oh, about ten to twenty years."

She said, "John Ed, you better give me that ring back or my mama and dad are going to come after you and me both."

Same thing with the fountain pen. The boy wouldn't let me keep it. See, even those kids knew that I didn't really own that ring or that pen. They had just been entrusted to me so I could use them for a minute. Like a lot of us with God's money, though, I decided I'd rather just hang on to something that wasn't really mine, and that's when the problems began.

> ## The hardest thing is to take less when you can get more.
> **—Kin Hubbard**

Let me put it another way. Do you have a daughter? If a boy comes to your house to date your daughter, I hope you don't let the boy assume he owns her and can do anything he wants to with her. I hope he has a sense that you're allowing him to go out with her, and that he needs to be a good steward of that relationship.

Or let's say you send your son off to college. I hope you don't let the college assume it owns your son. I hope you don't let them say, "Hey, we'll indoctrinate him any way we want to." No, that college has stewardship of training.

One more example: If you decide to let me borrow your car, I hope you don't let me assume it's mine. If I want to run it into the side of the building, I'll do it, right? Well, no. It's not mine, so I need to take care of it.

God gives abundantly

In the same way, not a single penny that God gives us is our own, so we shouldn't assume it's ours. Rather, he gave it to us from his own hand. He entrusts it to us, and expects us to be wise about remembering where it came from.

In Deuteronomy 8:10–18, Moses was talking to the Israelites. He had just given them the Ten Commandments, and was reminding them of God's goodness as they prepared to enter the promised land. Listen to his warning:

> When you have eaten your fill, praise the LORD your God for the good land he has given you.

> But that is the time to be careful! Beware that in your plenty you do not forget the LORD your God and disobey his commands, regulations, and laws. For when you have become full and prosperous and have built fine homes to live in, and when your flocks and herds have become very large and your silver and gold have multiplied along with every-thing else, that is the time to be careful. Do not become proud at that time and forget the LORD your God, who rescued you from slavery in the land of Egypt. Do not forget that he led you through the great and terrifying wilderness with poisonous snakes and scorpions, where it was so hot and dry. He gave you water from the rock! He fed you with manna in the wilderness, a food unknown to your ancestors. He did this to humble you and test you for your own good.

He did it so you would never think that it was your own strength and energy that made you wealthy. Always remember that it is the LORD your God who gives you power to become rich, and he does it to fulfill the covenant he made with your ancestors.

keeping perspective

The Bible is full of stories about people who have abundantly received but have misplaced their priorities in the process. They started thinking they had it together, and in the process, forgot how much they really needed God.

> You make a living by what you get.
> You make a life by what you give.
> **—Winston Churchill**

There was Adam, who certainly had everything he ever needed in the Garden of Eden, but fell to Satan's temptation regardless. There was Noah. After the flood, which wiped out virtually everyone else, he and his family pretty much owned it all. But he ended up drinking too much. And then there was David, who enjoyed great success as the leader of a prosperous nation, but risked it all by committing adultery and having the woman's husband killed.

If they can forget God's providence, it can just as easily happen to us. Read on in Deuteronomy 8:19–20:

If you ever forget the LORD your God and follow other gods, worshiping and bowing down to them, you will certainly be destroyed. Just as the LORD has destroyed other nations in your path, you also will be destroyed for not obeying the LORD your God.

That sounds pretty harsh, but it shows that God takes this seriously. We're not to forget that everything we have comes directly from him. And when we begin to understand that, that's when we find the motivation to give it back.

As we've seen, success can sometimes be the worst thing that happens to us, because we can lose sight of what's really important. On the other hand, success can also bring great opportunities. When we realize that we use our money to further God's kingdom on earth and to bless those around us, that's when things get exciting. That's also when God wants to give us more and more.

When we give money, it's a tangible demonstration that God has first place in our lives. It says we trust him to provide for us, and that we know if we give as we are led, he's still going to make sure we have what we need, too.

eternal reward

We can talk a lot, we can philosophize a lot, and we can rationalize a lot; but when it comes down to it, the place I put my money determines my priorities more than anything else. It's often said that we can check our hearts by checking our checkbooks, and that's so true. Are we spending our money on the things that are here and now, the things that will rot away?

Luke 16:1–12 tells a great story about a rich man who hires a manager to handle his affairs. The men had their differences, and the manager was about to be let go. So he devised a plan to ensure that he would still have plenty of friends to take care of him if he did indeed lose his job. He went around to the people who owed his boss money, telling them to tear up their bills and only pay a fraction of what was originally owed. The rich man, we're told in verse 8, "had to admire the dishonest rascal for being so shrewd." In verses 8–11, Jesus continued:

> And it is true that the citizens of this world are more shrewd than the godly are. I tell you, use your worldly resources to benefit others and make friends. In this way, your generosity stores up a reward for you in heaven. Unless you are faithful in small matters, you won't be faithful in large ones. If you

cheat even a little, you won't be honest with greater responsibilities. And if you are untrustworthy about worldly wealth, who will trust you with the true riches of heaven? And if you are not faithful with other people's money, why should you be trusted with money of your own?

It's my hope that we could all be trusted with money of our own. And the only way that can happen is for us to be conscious of how we spend what we already have, being willing to use it for the Kingdom instead of just for ourselves. As Jesus reminds us in Luke 16:13, we can't serve both God and money. And when it comes down to a choice, I've never heard of money being a very good master.

dive in

- *What does my checkbook say about my priorities?*
- *How can I make sure I don't forget the things God has given me?*
- *Has there ever been a time that money has been my god?*

It isn't the size of the gift that matters,
but the size of the heart that gives it.
  —*Eileen Elias Freeman*

facts and figures

Three men were talking one day about how much they gave to God. They all knew they were supposed to give, but they had different ways of figuring out how much. The first one said, "I'll tell you what I do. I take all my money and put it in my pocket. Then I stand up, and draw a circle around me about two feet in diameter. Next, I take all the money in my pocket and throw it up in the air. When it comes down, what lands in the circle is God's, and what lands outside of it is mine."

The second one said, "Hey, I do better than that. I stand in a circle like that and throw all my money up in the air, too. But what lands outside the circle is God's and what lands inside is mine." They looked at the third fellow, and one of them asked, "What about you? What do you do?"

He said, "I do the same thing. I draw a circle. Then I get inside it and throw all the money up and say, 'God, whatever you want, you just keep up there,' and then whatever comes down, I know he wants me to have."

tithe is 10 percent

Obviously, there are many ways to look at the subject of how much we're supposed to give to God. But I'd like to look at what the Bible says, and that's where you'll find a principle called the tithe. Some people mistakenly think that a tithe is just whatever you give, no matter how much that is. But that's not quite right. A tithe is very specifically 10 percent of what we take in, and gifts are anything beyond that expected tenth. It doesn't matter how much or how little we actually make; a tithe is still supposed to be 10 percent. Now, we're living in a world today in which athletes can earn a ton of money. But you know what gets me really excited about that? When I hear about the ones who give a tenth of it back to God, no matter how much it is. Now, it's one thing to think about giving God $5,000 a year for a $50,000 year salary. But what if your salary is in the millions?

God is the owner and you are the ower.
This puts God in his place and you in yours.
You are not free to manage your material
possessions as you like, but as he likes.

—E. Stanley Jones

Barry Sanders, the celebrated running back of the Detroit Lions, is said to have given a tenth of his more than two-million-dollar signing bonus to his church in Kansas. When asked why he did it, he simply said, "Because the Bible says you should tithe." It's also been said that he continued to give a tithe throughout the rest of his football career.

it's all about obedience

Contrast that with the widow in Mark 12:42–44 who puts only two pennies into the offering plate. Jesus tells the disciples that she gave "more than all the others have given. For they gave a tiny part of their surplus, but she, poor as she is, has given everything she has."

See, tithing is not about the actual amount of money. It's about the amount of obedience. The widow gave not what was in her pocketbook, but rather, what was in her heart.

When I was kid, the first job I had was to deliver the newspaper. Every morning, I got up and threw those papers before I went to school. It was tough.

I'll never forget my first paycheck. When I got it, my dad said, "Now, John Ed, the first tenth goes to the church." I said, "Dad, I'm going to start that real soon. There's this baseball glove . . ."

And he said, "John Ed, the tithe comes first, and when you put that in front, you'll find you have plenty for anything else." I'm so glad that I had parents that taught me that. They also taught me that the tithe—the 10 percent—was the minimum. We don't really give anything to God until we go beyond that.

So where do we get the idea of 10 percent? It comes from the twenty-seventh chapter of Leviticus. That's where Moses told the people in verse 30 that "a tenth of the produce of the land, whether grain or fruit, belongs to the LORD and must be set apart to him as holy." In addition, verse 32 says, "The LORD also owns every tenth animal counted off from your herds and flocks. They are to be set apart to him as holy."

It's a good thing God made it easy on us—especially those of us who aren't good at math. He didn't instruct us to tithe 8 percent or 12 percent; he said 10. And that should be easy enough to figure out.

When Moses was talking to the Israelites about the tithe, he also addressed the people who wanted to give more than the 10 percent. For those people, he had a warning. Moses told them that if they were going to make promises to God, they shouldn't take those promises lightly. Otherwise, it could end up costing them more than they could have imagined. Someone who wanted to take back the Lord's tenth of the fruit or grain, for example, would have to pay its value plus 20 percent. In other words, Moses was saying, do the math and count the costs.

We should give as we would receive, cheerfully, quickly, and without hesitation; for there is no grace in a benefit that sticks to the fingers.

—Seneca

If you commit to tithe that 10 percent, God expects you to do it, no matter what other bills or opportunities come your way. There's no doubt that Satan will try to steal that money from you and give you all sorts of suggestions for what it could be better spent on. But hold firm; that tithe is a command.

A man recently called and said he had to meet with me. Well, that particular day was a busy one, so I asked if the next day would be OK. And he said no, he needed to see me that day. I said, "Well, OK. Maybe this afternoon?" But he said, "How about right now?"

I figured it must be something really important, so I said, "Sure. If it's that urgent, come on in." So he did, and here's what he told me: "I'm in transition between jobs right now. But I've made an investment, it paid off, and I got this check three days ago. Now, as a Christian, I know that a tenth of it belongs to the church. But Satan's been working on me since I don't have a job. I just can't wait until Sunday to put it in the offering plate, because Satan's after me. I couldn't even sleep last night. So would you take this check right now?"

I don't know what the amount was on that check. I don't know if it was a little or a lot. I never looked at it, in fact, because I don't ever want to know what anybody in the congregation gives. But that man, he said, "Whew. That's a relief. If I'd had to wait until Sunday, I know that Satan would have talked me out of giving it."

I heard a story about a man who got paid weekly and came by the church every Friday to turn in his tithe. One day the church secretary asked him why he did it that way. He responded, "Because I might die tomorrow. I don't want to die with any of God's money in my pocket."

What a different place the world could be if we truly understood the concept of God's money in our pockets! The unfortunate thing is that a lot of people in the church just don't take it seriously. Churches get used to making do, when they could be doing so much more.

put God first

Now, as a pastor myself, I wish I could take every member of the church and say, "Your language needs to be Christian. Your attitude needs to be Christian. You need to follow Jesus completely." I wish I could make you do that. I wish I could make every mother and father spend time with their kids and be godly parents. I wish I could make every husband and wife love each other like Christ loved the church. And when it comes to tithing, I wish I could make every person do that, too. But just like all the other things, it's an individual choice. I can't make you speak a certain way, or act towards your family or coworkers a certain way.

All I can do is encourage you to give it a shot. I promise you that if you do as God has said to do, he's going to bless you for it. Now, I challenge you to think about what giving a tenth of your income would really mean. Sometimes Christians say they'll do it if they have enough left over, but the truth is, that's rarely going to happen. The key, then, is to give that tithe first, so you don't even miss it. The key is to remember that by giving it, we're honoring the command of Exodus 20:3 that tells us we shouldn't have any other gods before him—and that money is not god in our lives.

offerings

If you ever decide to give more than that tenth, some churches call that a gift, and some churches call it an offering. We can give both tithes and offerings, and I want to be clear that they're not the same thing. What often happens, though, is that people start with the tithe, and find that they receive so much in return that they begin to give more and more. The return blessings are more than just financial; God changes something on the inside.

If you haven't any charity in your heart, you have the worst kind of heart trouble.

—Bob Hope

An exceptional example of that comes through a Texas businessman named R. G. LeTourneau. He was an industrialist on a grand scale, who made himself a nice little fortune. He was outspoken in his devotion to God, and began tithing at 10 percent. Before long, he was giving 20 percent. And then 40, 60, and finally, 90 percent, much of it going toward missionary work. Even when his business wasn't doing so well, he still gave sacrificially. And quite famously, he said, "The question is not how much of my money I give to God, but rather how much of God's money I keep for myself."

Now that's a picture of an offering that's about more than just money. That's an offering of a life. Remember: It's not about the numbers; it's about the heart. And 10 percent is a good place to start opening it up.

dive in

- *How do I feel about the idea of committing 10 percent of my income to the church?*
- *Has God ever rewarded me for being generous?*
- *What keeps people from giving more to God?*

The Lord loveth a cheerful giver.
He also accepteth from a grouch.

—Catherine Hall

chapter 26

a cheerful giver

King David had been busy. Using every resource at his command, he had gathered as many materials as he could to help his son, Solomon, build a Temple to honor God. He had wanted to build it himself, but since he had been a warrior and had shed blood, God denied his request. The task, then, fell to Solomon, and David's task became the preparation.

Now, the Temple was to be an incredibly grand structure. David made all the arrangements for the young and inexperienced Solomon to oversee, and had gathered large quantities of gold, silver, bronze, iron, wood, onyx, turquoise, stones of various colors, and marble. But it wasn't enough.

In 1 Chronicles 29:3, we see him making a different kind of commitment to the project. He told the people:

> And now, because of my devotion to the Temple of my God,
> I am giving all of my own private treasures of gold and silver
> to help in the construction. This is in addition to the building
> materials I have already collected for his holy Temple.

His list of donations included more than 112 tons of gold and more than 262 tons of refined silver. Then he quite simply asked, "Now then, who will follow my example? Who is willing to give offerings to the LORD today?"

The response was just as he had hoped. The people gave willingly, freely, and wholeheartedly, so the work could be done. And King David, in return, openly praised God. He said in verses 13–15:

> O our God, we thank you and praise your glorious name! But who am I, and who are my people, that we could give anything to you? Everything we have has come from you, and we give you only what you have already given us!

At that point, his prayer took a turn. The next thing he said was, "We are here for only a moment, visitors and strangers in the land as our ancestors were before us. Our days on earth are like a shadow, gone so soon without a trace."

Isn't that the truth? Our opportunities on earth to do great things for God go by so quickly. Who are we, then, to not give it all we have while we can?

No one has ever become poor by giving.

—Anne Frank

As we've talked about giving, you may have considered becoming more generous with your gifts to the church and to others. If so, that's great. It's a commitment that God will honor. Others of us may be feeling uncomfortable and not yet ready to completely trust God with our finances. If you're feeling like that, I encourage you to start asking God for direction and wisdom concerning your giving. And I want all of us to take it a step further. God doesn't just call us to give. He calls us to give as David did: joyfully, purposefully, sacrificially, and expectantly.

There's a popular Sunday school lesson about a flint, a sponge, and a honeycomb. Those three things are supposed to represent the different kinds of givers there are in the world. First, there's the flint. To get anything out of the flint, you've got to hammer it, and it's likely to give off sparks when you do. Next is the sponge; the more you squeeze, the more you get—but you've still got to squeeze it. And finally, there's the honeycomb. That's the one that overflows with its own sweetness. That's the kind of giver God is, and the kind we can be, too.

What does it take to get there? Let's start with a quick science lesson. In 2 Corinthians 9:6, we're reminded that a farmer who plants only a few seeds will end up with a small crop. "But the one who plants generously will get a generous crop." We can't expect a bountiful harvest if we're not willing to plant the seeds. In the same way, we can't hoard our own money yet expect God to still be generous with us.

Now, in the next verse, Paul continued, "You must each make up your own mind as to how much you should give. Don't give reluctantly or in response to pressure. For God loves the person who gives cheerfully," or as most of us have heard it quoted, "God loves a cheerful giver."

God also loves the person who gives sacrificially. In 1 Kings 17, we're told the story of a poor widow who lived with her son. It was during a famine, and the prophet Elijah was told to go see the woman for some food.

She was busy outside when Elijah arrived, and he asked her for a cup of water and a bite of bread. But she responded in verse 12:

> I swear by the LORD your God that I don't have a single piece of bread in the house. And I have only a handful of flour left in the jar and a little cooking oil in the bottom of the jug. I was just gathering a few sticks to cook this last meal, and then my son and I will die.

Elijah's response was this:

Don't be afraid! Go ahead and cook that "last meal," but bake me a little loaf of bread first. Afterward there will still be enough food for you and your son. For this is what the LORD, the God of Israel, says: There will always be plenty of flour and oil left in your containers until the time when the LORD sends rain and the crops grow again!

The widow took a risk. She chose to give sacrificially to feed the prophet, and as a result, she and her son had enough flour and oil for many days to come. No matter how much they used, there was always more in the containers, just as God promised through Elijah.

It would be easy to read this story and think that woman was paid back for her trouble, that she had already received her reward. But God just kept on giving in return. Some time later, we learn in verse 17, the woman's son became sick and died. Elijah carried him up to the upper room of the house where he had been staying and prayed for him. God heard Elijah's prayer and brought him back to life.

Little did that widow know, when she sacrificially gave to the prophet, what kind of rewards would be in store for her. And it works the same way with us. When we give, we have no idea what God will do next.

obedience rewarded

A woman in our congregation told me a story about how she began to tithe. At first, she was reluctant and did it simply out of obedience. Before long, her attitude changed to one of giving out of joy. Do you know what happened next? Within a year, her salary had doubled. As she saw what God had done with what she had given, she was that much more excited about giving the next time.

I encourage people to share their testimonies about what God has done through their willingness to give. It's so important for us to remember and share these stories, because they encourage us to keep at it. They also help us remember that it's not really our money that God wants. It's us.

There once was a granddaddy who gave his grandson ten one-dollar bills for Christmas. He watched intently as the boy took them out. The granddaddy said, "What are going to do with that?"

The little boy responded, "Well, the first one, that's my tithe. That goes to Jesus." Now, that granddaddy was impressed. The boy went on. He described the things he wanted to do with the other dollars, and when he got to the last one, he said, "This one goes to Jesus, too."

The granddaddy said, "Well, you've already given Jesus the tenth."

His grandson responded, "Yes, sir, that's my tithe. But this is my present because I love him." He had it exactly right. He gave not because he had to, but because he wanted to.

Let me tell you, though, where Satan comes into our lives. He comes in and says things like, "You don't really need to give as much as you do. Go ahead and keep it." We may be tempted, but we shouldn't give in. If we put God first, everything else has a way of lining up behind him.

God has a plan

You may have heard this story about a midwestern church that lost its treasurer. The leaders thought that the manager of a local grain elevator would be right for the job, and approached him about the position. After some consideration, the manager agreed to the job for a year, as long as nobody questioned him about the church's finances throughout that time. They thought it was kind of an odd condition, but they knew him to be a trustworthy man through his business, so they agreed.

What a year it turned out to be! At the end of it, when the treasurer gave his report, he said the building had been paid off, the pastor's salary had been increased, all the bills were covered, and there was even a surplus in the bank. Obviously, the church leaders were surprised, and they asked the treasurer how he had pulled it off.

> # I do not believe one can settle how much we ought to give. . . . The only safe rule is to give more than we can spare.
> **—C. S. Lewis**

Many of the church members brought him grain throughout the year, he explained. When they did, the manager withheld 10 percent of what he would have paid them, and gave it to the church in their name. "See what happens," he asked, "when everybody gives?"

Of course, that's just a story. Preachers can't do that; we can't make people give. But we can hope and pray that they will give so willingly, for their own benefit as much as anything else. I hope you'll be on the receiving end of someone else's generosity, too.

receive gracefully

My wife and I had a wonderful experience some time ago. We had traveled to Gatlinburg, Tennessee, where I was speaking to an older adult assembly. After the session was over, we went to eat in a nearby restaurant. We were sitting at a table by the window, watching the tourists go by, when a young gentleman wearing a baseball cap—I'm going to say he was in his late twenties—came up and tapped me on the back.

He said, "Dr. Mathison, man, you don't know what your ministry means to me. We tape your television show when we can't see it." He said his wife was outside, then pointed to a young lady sitting on a bench who looked like a college cheerleader, just smiling away. He said, "We're on vacation, and we just saw you sitting here. I'm an evangelist."

Now, young evangelists don't have a whole lot. But he went on. "She and I just decided that we want to buy supper for you and your wife." He then put down a hundred-dollar bill. We could have eaten at that restaurant four times and not eaten one hundred dollars' worth. Before I could get up and say something, he said, "No, no. Give me the privilege of doing this." And he was gone.

I know he couldn't afford that. But sacrificially, joyfully, he wanted to share something with us, and we were blessed. I gave that one-hundred-dollar bill to my wife, and said, "Look, you take it and go buy something with it." She replied, "No, let's just keep it." So I still have it, and it serves as a reminder about giving and receiving and the impact it can have on someone else.

Always remember that money can soon be gone, just like our days on earth, as King David said. I hear people say, "I'm going to start doing all this later on," but there may not be any later on. Don't presume on the future. We have a lot of funerals at our church, and we've never had one yet where they allowed a U-Haul to be hooked up to the back of the church, carrying what the person wasn't yet ready to release.

dive in

- *If I had to use an adjective to describe my giving, what would it be?*
- *If Elijah had come to my house, asking for water and bread, how would I have responded?*
- *What difference does it make to God whether I give cheerfully or begrudgingly?*

A closed hand can't receive.

—*Author Unknown*

chapter 27

faith is rewarded

I read a story about how monkeys are captured in the wild. First of all, the people start with a gourd and put a small hole in the top of it. Then they put seeds in the top and tie the thing to a stake in the ground.

The monkey comes along and sees the seeds, and since the opening is big enough for his hand, he reaches inside. But when he grasps the seeds and closes his fist, he can't get it out.

Do you know what happens? The monkey won't let go. All he has to do is release what's in his hand, and he can be free. But he won't. He'll continue to hang on to those seeds, even until those people come and capture him.

The truth is, anything that we hold that tightly—money or otherwise—is certain to trap us sooner or later. It is only by letting go that we can really be free.

There's one more thing about money that we really ought to cover, and that's what happens when people give. Yes, we've talked about God's promises to bless us and take care of us, as well as how our selflessness can provide an example that leads other people to Jesus. But there's more.

Giving doesn't drain stagnant places in our lives. Instead, it turns them into rushing rivers. It can make all the difference between just getting by and flourishing. When people are just getting by and they're in that stagnant spot in their finances, they seek relief. Even if it's just for a little while. They're kind of like people in the desert; they want shelter, and they crave refreshment.

Interestingly enough, a generous heart can take care of both. We can find shelter in the fact that God takes care of our business when we take care of his. He makes sure our needs are met as we meet the needs of others, just as we saw in that story of the widow and her unending supply of oil.

Look at Luke 6:38:

> If you give, you will receive. Your gift will return to you in full measure, pressed down, shaken together to make room for more, and running over. Whatever measure you use in giving—large or small—it will be used to measure what is given back to you.

As for craving refreshment, that comes when we take our eyes off ourselves for a while and focus on someone else. The surest way to put our own problems in perspective is to start listening to other people share theirs. In order for this giving concept to work, we have to be willing to see what's around us—as well as what's above us. The more we release, then, the more aware we become.

Have you ever watched a group of pigs? Pigs never look up. All they do is keep their head down and look for another acorn or another nut. They never look up to give thanks for where those nuts and acorns come from.

Unfortunately, a lot of us are like those pigs. We go through life looking for what we can get, and never bother to look up and say thank you. And when we're looking down, all we see is what's there. We have no idea what's coming, and we're more apt to complain. But when we're looking up, we're more likely to give thanks; maybe it's because we can see that nuts are about to fall our way.

> Be not anxious about what you have,
> but about what you are.
>
> **—St. Gregory the Great**

One of the great basketball players years ago was Bill Bradley. He's a former U.S. Senator now, but I got to know him at Princeton. Bradley went on to play with the New York Knicks and led them to a couple of world championship titles.

Bradley was the subject of a book called *A Sense of Where You Are*. Whenever he played basketball, he had a sense of where everybody was on the court. The thing that made him great, they said, was that he had such great peripheral vision. It's been said that he could look straight ahead and still see everybody on the court. He was actually tested for his peripheral vision, as well as his vertical vision. The people doing the tests discovered that he was exceptional in both. Bradley could actually see the basket while looking at the floor.

The rest of us aren't quite built that way. So we have to ask, how's our horizontal vision? How aware are we of the needs of the people around us? And how's our vertical vision? How willing are we to actually lift our heads and look up to where our blessings are coming from?

When our eyes look to God, our hearts begin to change. As you ask him to guide you more and more, and listen to what he tells you to do, he takes you on a great adventure, and it gets to be a lot of fun wondering what he's going to do next. You might feel led to give somebody a certain amount of money, and it will turn out to be exactly what they needed. You might feel led to buy a person a particular gift, and it could turn out to be exactly what they wanted.

And you might feel led to go beyond giving that 10 percent weekly tithe to the church, and it could open your eyes to the ways God stretches money in the hands of the faithful. Read this passage from Matthew 6:25–33:

> So I tell you, don't worry about everyday life—whether you have enough food, drink, and clothes. Doesn't life consist of more than food and clothing? Look at the birds. They don't need to plant or harvest or put food in barns because your heavenly Father feeds them. And you are far more valuable to him than they are. Can all your worries add a single moment to your life? Of course not. And why worry about your clothes? Look at the lilies and how they grow. They don't work or make their clothing, yet Solomon in all his glory was not dressed as beautifully as they are. And if God cares so wonderfully for flowers that are here today and gone tomorrow, won't he more surely care for you? You have so little faith! So don't worry about having enough food or drink or clothing. Why be like the pagans who are so deeply concerned about these things? Your heavenly Father already knows all your needs, and he will give you all you need from day to day if you live for him and make the Kingdom of God your primary concern.

What a promise—and what a great way to live! That truly is a definition of freedom, being free from worries and concerns, knowing that we'll be well taken care of as long as we live for him. In this equation, we get back far more than we give.

wealth doesn't mean blessed

Now, as we're talking about giving, I want to caution against a couple of things. First is the idea that anybody who has any sort of wealth must be all right with God. That's not necessarily the case. It doesn't mean that they're being blessed, or that they live righteous lives. Luke 16:19–31 tells a story about two men: one is wealthy, and the other is a beggar. The beggar was in such poor shape that the dogs would come and lick his sores. He rested at the gate of the rich man, and longed to eat what fell from the rich man's table.

Both men eventually died. The rich man ended up in hell, however, and the beggar, in heaven. Even though the rich man had enough material possessions to help the beggar while both were still on earth, he chose not to, and the consequence of his selfishness and insensitivity was steep.

> ## Money will buy a pretty good dog, but it won't buy the wag of his tail.
> ### —Josh Billings

In the same way, there are a lot of very wealthy, very selfish people in our society. God may have allowed them to gain that wealth, but he may also be teaching them important life lessons through it. We never know the true state of another man's heart, but God does. In the same way, we can't judge someone who's going through a rough time financially, assuming that they must be doing something wrong. Again, God may be working out issues in that person's heart, preparing him or her for wealth that is to come.

do your duty

Now, as for those of us who regularly tithe and give offerings, we have to be careful that we don't let pride seep in, just because we're obeying God. When we obey him, we're only doing what's expected. Jesus puts it this way in Luke 17:7–10:

When a servant comes in from plowing or taking care of
sheep, he doesn't just sit down and eat. He must first prepare
his master's meal and serve him his supper before eating his
own. And the servant is not even thanked, because he is
merely doing what he is supposed to do. In the same way,
when you obey me you should say, "We are not worthy of
praise. We are servants who have simply done our duty."

And giving is indeed part of our duty. It will remain our duty
no matter how our wealth actually grows.

in God we trust

I once read about a preacher who had a very distraught man
come to him one day. He had been making $20,000, and had
been tithing on that. But his salary had since jumped to
$150,000. So he said to the pastor, he didn't know what to do,
because a tithe on $150,000 would simply be too much.

Do you know how that pastor responded? He said, "Let's
pray that God will put you back to making $20,000, when you
could really acknowledge who he was."

See, money can change us, and not always in a good way.
Fortunately, we always have the choice to open up our fists and
let our giving change us first. Here's what Paul has to say on the
subject in 1 Timothy 6:17–18:

Tell those who are rich in this world not to be proud and not
to trust in their money, which will soon be gone. But their
trust should be in the living God, who richly gives us all we
need for our enjoyment. Tell them to use their money to do
good. They should be rich in good works and should give
generously to those in need, always being ready to share with
others whatever God has given them.

The question remains: Are we going to be like those
monkeys who stick their hands in gourds and refuse to let go?
Or are we going to release the seeds in our hands and know that

they're only a fraction of what could be available to us as we walk in freedom? It's our choice, really. We can choose how blessed we'd like to be.

dive in

- *Have I ever seen God stretch my money?*
- *How close am I to that monkey with his fist caught inside the gourd?*
- *In what areas could I be more generous?*

*It's time for greatness—not for greed. It's a time for idealism
—not ideology. It is a time not just for compassionate words,
but compassionate action.*

—Marian Wright Edelman

chapter 28
riches beyond measure

Have you ever paid attention to what happens to lottery winners? Every so often, there's a story on the news about one or another. You'd think that winning a large sum of money would change their lives for the better, but it's not necessarily the case. Instead, past lottery winners often make the headlines for the second time when they go broke, pick up dangerous—or even illegal—habits, find themselves involved in lawsuits, and discover that they've lost total trust in everyone around them because everyone seems to have a hand out, looking for their share.

Money can be a tricky thing, whether there's a lot of it or a little of it. It's so easy to think that it can solve all of the world's problems, but it can't. I wonder how many people who ever won the lottery had prayed to win it, and how God decided to answer those prayers. I don't know how he decides who gets what, but I do know that God sees the end from the beginning, and he knows what we can handle and what we can't.

I'm reminded again of that story from Matthew 25:14–30, in which a man went on a trip and entrusted bags of gold to his servants. If you recall, two of the servants invested the money and pleased their master, but the third hid it in fear. There's something I've always wondered about this story: Why do you think the three servants were all entrusted with different amounts? Had they already proven their level of trustworthiness or ability? Did the master know that one of them would be foolish with his sum? Did he know the other two would be wise?

What does this say about our own financial state? Are we doing well with the small things so God can give us greater things? *Does the way I handle money motivate God to give me more?*

maintaining balance

Think about where you'd be without money in your life. How would you pay for your house? How would you put gas in your car, keep the lights turned on, and the refrigerator stocked?

It's the same way in God's house, too. The staff needs to be paid. The church bus gas tank must be filled, the lights kept on, and some money set aside to help those in distress. So where does that money come from? Psalm 50:10 tells us that God owns the cattle on a thousand hills, but he doesn't write a check every week to make sure those things are taken care of.

Just as with everything else we've discussed, God wants to partner with us to do it. Yes, he can do miracles in finances. He can give our church leaders wisdom on where to invest and how to stretch a dollar. He wants to use us, however, to finance his work.

Am I cheating God, or do I acknowledge how much he's given me by how much I give back?

heavenly treasure

Just as with the rich young man in Luke 18:18–30, money and our attitude toward it reveal a lot about our faith in God.

The young man had already jumped through a dozen hoops in his effort to attain eternal life; but giving away everything he had was his line in the sand. He wouldn't, or couldn't, do that even if it meant giving up eternal life. He wanted eternal life enough to do good things, but he didn't want it enough to give up some of the comforts of his earthly life.

Can't we be the same way? Sometimes we're afraid that if we give, we won't have enough to cover the electric bill or make the house payment. We like to write the tithe check out of what's left when we've paid every other bill that must be paid. And there will be many, many times when there's nothing left over.

But if we hold on tightly to what we have out of fear, do we really give God room to work?

Remember what God says in Malachi 3:10 (NIV): "Test me in this." If we give God his portion first, do we have a chance to see a miracle in all the bills getting paid anyway? If we give sacrificially, do we give God a chance to blow us away with his blessing?

Do I focus more on my own fears about not having enough, or on God's ability to take care of me?

keeping priorities in line

We tithe because we're commanded to, plain and simple. God's Word is extremely clear on that point. When we don't tithe, we're told that we're cheating God. We're told that we're serving money as a master if we put it before God. So why would we want to give more than a tithe? Let's hope that it's for the same reasons we give Christmas and birthday gifts: because we have an overwhelming love for the person on the receiving end.

In the world, we can get that all messed up. Sometimes we give gifts out of obligation, or because we think the recipient might have something for us in return. You may have even heard about bridal couples who figure that each wedding guest should give a gift that's at least equal to the per-person cost of the reception. You've seen the TV ads that tell a man that his engagement ring should equal three months' salary. You've also probably heard of newly engaged women who take those rings to be appraised so they can see how much their fiancés think they're worth.

Each Christmas season, analysts predict how much money each family will spend on holiday gifts. A study in 2005 showed that the average pet owner would spend one hundred dollars on Christmas gifts for his or her pets. It's sad to say, but of all the gifts we give, the ones we give our pets may just be the most unconditional.

We've gotten our gift-giving out of whack. We give because we think we'll get something in return. We measure the worth of the gift and ignore the adage about the thought being what counts.

Are we that way in our gift-giving to God? Do we give because we think we'll get something in return? If not a financial blessing from God, then at least acknowledgment from the pastor? Do we give out of obligation? Do we give foolishly into foolish pursuits? Or do we give to God because of our overwhelming appreciation for what he's done for us?

What does my giving reveal about my heart?

facts and figures

So, if giving is good, then I should give more than God asks, right? Remember, giving isn't about a dollar figure as much as it is about obedience. Sometimes God will lead us to give a gift that exceeds our tithe by a number of zeroes. And sometimes, he'll tell us not to give anything more than the tithe.

Yes, that's right. God will sometimes tell us not to give, even though our hearts may have been touched by the plea or moved by the particular situation. Are we willing to be obedient to God in those circumstances, too?

Understand that there will always be more needs than we are called to meet. Even Jesus says we'll always have the poor. Just as when the woman broke the expensive bottle of perfume over Jesus' feet, sometimes we need to lavish our love on God rather than meeting the needs of our fellow humans. Sometimes we do that best by our obedience.

As we mature with money, we need to learn to hear God's voice regarding what and when to give. Perhaps you think God is telling you to give a homeless man five dollars, but you think he'll probably only use it to buy liquor, so you don't want to give. Regardless, obedience is always the better choice; what the man does with the money is between him and God. You're only accountable for you.

But what about a circumstance in which God tells you to give that same homeless man five dollars and you pull out a ten-dollar-bill? Don't do it. Following God's direction when we give—or don't give—is another way of acknowledging that we're merely stewards of all that God has given us. Giving too much can be just as wrong as giving too little.

Am I willing to allow God to tell me how much to give? Am I willing to give boldly when God allows, and to hold back my offerings when God leads that direction, too?

a cheerful giver

We often use the story of Cain and Abel to illustrate what happens when we have hatred in our heart for someone. But do you know what was at the root of their disagreement? It was the giving of their tithes.

In Genesis 4:3, Abel gave some of his sheep to God; he had carefully picked through his flock to find the best ones. Cain's offering was from his crops. Many have interpreted this to mean that rather than pick the best, he offered the stuff that had already fallen to the ground. Do you know what happens when fruit falls to the ground? It's usually past its prime and is starting to rot. The fall itself may have bruised the fruit, and animals may even have gnawed on it. Cain was hardly giving God his best. Instead, he was offering what he didn't need or couldn't use.

God accepts Abel's gift, but he rejects Cain's. In verse 7, he even warns Cain that "sin is waiting to attack and destroy you." And attack, it does. You know the rest of the story about the two brothers: Cain murdered Abel and roamed the earth hiding from God.

God loves a cheerful giver. And don't you think that was the root of Cain's problem? He wanted the best for himself and chose to give God the leftovers. Do we do that with our giving? Do we shortchange God by arguing over whether to give our tithe based on gross or net? Do we round down instead of rounding up? Do we try to justify not tithing on certain things?

Do I give tithes cheerfully, or do I look for loopholes?

riches beyond measure

When we give, we give God the opportunity to do the miraculous. When we give to a missionary, we provide the opportunity for someone to hear the miraculous salvation message. When we give to the benevolence ministry, we help provide the miracle of food, shoes, or electricity.

When we give, we also offer God the opportunity to do a miracle for us. Remember the widow who had almost no food, but gave to the prophet? God provided a miracle for her that no amount of money could buy.

But mostly, when we give, we receive the miracle of being able to decrease while God increases in our lives. We receive the miracle of putting our own needs and wants aside in favor of God's ways. We die to our own selfishness a little bit each time we write a tithe check. And the more we die to ourselves, the more we become like him.

Granted, that could be reward enough. But it's not all he offers. Remember the monkey that wouldn't let go? He thought the biggest reward he could receive was that pitiful little handful of seeds. And yet, by releasing his grasp, he could have been rewarded with something much greater: his very life. It's the same way with us. We might think that what's already in our grasp is as precious as it gets. We have no idea how richly God can reward us when we show a little faith.

How tightly do I cling to the things that will soon pass away? Can God trust me with his resources?

offering a drink
to others

chapter 29

imitate Christ

I've got a challenge for you: Can you come up with a synonym for water? I bet not.

There are words that mean the same thing as the verb form, such as "to irrigate," "to wet," or "to run," as in the case with tears. But when it comes to the noun form, the essence of the stuff itself, it's no easy task.

That could be because there really is no substitute. Nothing even comes close. That's especially true when it comes to living things. Doctors tell us that, as humans, we're about 60 percent water. The brain is actually comprised of 75 percent water, and the blood, 82 percent. As such, we can go about forty days without food, but only three days without water. Then we die.

The Body of Christ, interestingly enough, is the same way. We, too, need to be refreshed and sustained. We need lubrication in our joints to improve flexibility, fuel for our muscles to increase strength, and movement in our blood so the heart remains connected to the brain.

In the case of the Body of Christ, I believe service is the water that does all that and more. Reaching out in service to others really does make us more flexible, helps us strengthen our gifts, and reminds us that God is constantly at work around us. But it does something else that may be the most important part of all: It allows us to be more like Jesus.

seeing the need

The Bible offers us story after story about what kind of servant Jesus was and the many things he selflessly did for other people while on earth. He healed. He loved. He fed. He washed feet. He carried a cross.

Reading these stories, we find that Jesus willingly volunteered. As he said in Matthew 20:28: "I, the Son of Man, came here not to be served, but to serve others, and to give my life as a ransom for many." He didn't have to be recruited to make a blind man see or a lame man walk. He simply saw need and found ways to meet it.

How different the church would be today if we would follow the same principle. Many congregations, unfortunately, find they have to recruit people to get them to serve. No telling how much time is wasted trying to figure out who the best person might be for the job. No telling how much more we could accomplish if we weren't just sitting around, waiting to be asked.

> In giving you are throwing a bridge across the chasm of your solitude.
>
> **—Antoine de Saint-Exupéry**

All this, of course, goes against the way the world thinks. We're taught to put ourselves first, and then to worry about others. We're taught that the way up the ladder of success is to step on other people to get there. But here's what Jesus said in Matthew 20:25:

You know that in this world kings are tyrants, and officials lord it over the people beneath them. But among you it should be quite different. Whoever wants to be a leader among you must be your servant, and whoever wants to be first must become your slave.

This isn't just about the one serving and the one being served, though. A lifestyle of service gives us credibility with others as true messengers for Christ. When we love other people enough to do things for them without expecting anything in return, they see that what we believe is counter to anything the world has to offer. From there, it's a natural progression to show that God loves us in the same way: completely and unconditionally. The most impressive witnesses are those who first serve in some way, earning the right to be heard when they share the gospel. As it's often been said, "Preach the gospel at all times. Use words if necessary."

reaching out in love

A servant attitude can help bring people into God's family and also bring unity to the family that's already there. Under the direction of Christ, the apostle Paul wrote in Ephesians 4:15–16:

The whole body is fitted together perfectly. As each part does its own special work, it helps the other parts grow, so that the whole body is healthy and growing and full of love.

A friend of mine has a great story about someone who did a nice thing for him when he was a kid. It had such an impact that he remembers it clearly even now.

When John was about eleven, he went to the hospital to have his appendix removed. In those days, when you had that done, you stayed in the hospital for a whole week with no TV, video games, or anything. You can imagine how awful an experience that would have been for an eleven-year-old.

Since the hospital wasn't too fond of kids hanging around, John's friends couldn't visit during his stay. One of them snuck into the hospital anyway, and brought an entire backpack of games with him. John's friend spent an entire day there. He'd keep a lookout for any nurses, and any time they appeared, he'd slide into a closet or under the bed to hide.

As John said, "I don't even know what kind of trouble he got in. I don't know if his parents knew where he was. But I knew this: He wanted to be with me that day. That meant a ton to me."

Admittedly, John's friend probably enjoyed some of the adventure of sneaking into the hospital as much as anything. But even at eleven, he understood something that others of us take much longer to comprehend: Reaching out in love—being there for someone else—is usually worth the risk.

I say "risk" because there is, indeed, risk involved with serving. We have to let go of pride and ego to do it, or else it won't really do what it's supposed to do. "Unless the LORD builds a house, the work of the builders is useless," as we're told in Psalm 127:1.

Everybody can be great.
Because anybody can serve.
—Martin Luther King Jr.

I'll be honest; when we reach out to someone else, several things can happen. The person on the receiving end might reject us. They may not appreciate what we do for them. We might receive no recognition at all. Ultimately, though, that's not what being a servant is about. Rather, it's about doing the right thing, no matter how it's received.

side effects

When a church has every member serving together, there is little desire to complain or gossip or be divisive. As my dad likes to say, "You can't row the boat and rock it at the same time." It's only when the whole congregation rows that the church actually gets somewhere, and it's only when that happens that everybody is being blessed.

I'll tell you a secret: Even though we're not supposed to serve thinking we'll get something in return, God has a way of working things out. And his rewards are incredible.

One of our church members told a story about how he had decided to serve others by giving blood. He hadn't given blood in a long time, but because of this decision, he went to the clinic. The technician who took his blood told him that he should go to see his doctor.

He went to his doctor the next day and discovered that he had an early form of a fast-growing cancer. Since the doctors caught it so early, however, he was able to be treated. His doctor actually said, "If you hadn't come when you did, you wouldn't have been alive very long."

Don't take that story to mean that every time you serve, it's going to be a life-changing event. Do take it to mean, though, that serving can help lead you into a life that's more fulfilling and exciting than ever before. Because serving others allows us to get our eyes off ourselves and put them on God and others.

Going back to our analogy of water, one of the things water does for the body is to help it flush out toxins. In the context of the church body, the water of service does the same thing. It helps rid us of self-centeredness and wrong motives.

Water's also good for maintaining balance in the body's systems, and it helps carry essential nutrients from cell to cell. Are you making the connection? When we serve, we maintain the lifeblood of the church.

You've no doubt heard health experts telling us how much water we're supposed to drink to make up for what is expelled in the course of a day. Some experts even urge us to drink half our body weight in ounces of water each day. That may seem like a lot, but it gives you an idea of just how important water is to our bodies. Notice that those experts say to do this every day.

We're not camels; we can't store up what we need for long periods of time. Instead, to keep our bodies running smoothly, we're supposed to go back to that source time and again, day after day.

do what you can

Same thing with service. We can't just do one good deed and expect it to carry us through. We'll be so much better off if we're willing to look around us on a regular basis—just like Jesus did—and do whatever we can to help. That's the only way we can continue to humble our hearts before God and be used by him. Day after day, our prayer must be, "Lord, I'll go! Send me," just as it says in Isaiah 6:8.

Once God plants us in a place of consistent service, it's important that we give it all we've got, rather than spinning our wheels thinking about the next place we're going to go. You are extremely important, wherever you are. It's easy to say, "I wish I was someplace else." Sometimes preachers wish they were in other churches. Sometimes people in the congregation wish they were married, and others wish they were single. But we've got to remember that God puts us exactly where we are so he can use us the best way he knows how.

It is the greatest of all mistakes to do nothing because you can only do a little; do what you can.
—Sydney Smith

If you're the only Christian in your workplace, be glad. You've got a great mission field, and by reaching out to others, you can help the number of Christians there grow. If you're the only one in your circle who has a value system, that's wonderful. You've got a great opportunity to model humility and service.

It's all about changing the way we look at things, and being willing to put others in front of ourselves. It's all about bringing that water with us, and being willing to fill other people's cups to overflowing.

While we're looking around for places to serve, we might notice other people who seem more qualified or better suited to serve than we are. We may doubt our own abilities and wonder if we've got what it takes. But the next time you find yourself wishing you could do something someone else does or thinking that "the grass is always greener," consider this quote from author Robert Fulghum:

> The grass is not, in fact, always greener on the other side of the fence. Fences have nothing to do with it. The grass is greenest where it is watered. When crossing over the fences, carry water with you and tend the grass wherever you may be.

No doubt, it you're willing to look closely enough, you'll see parched grass all around.

dive in

- *What does the life of Jesus teach me about serving?*
- *When was the last time I reached out to someone with no thought of what I could get in return?*
- *What's my motivation for serving others?*

The world is a dangerous place, not because of those who do evil,
but because of those who look on and do nothing.
                                        —*Albert Einstein*

chapter 30

a life worthwhile

Ever heard of a guy named Albert Einstein?

Of course you have. Many have said he was the most brilliant man since Jesus. He was known for his theory of relativity and his contributions to the fields of quantum mechanics, statistical mechanics, and cosmology, among others. For a long time, Einstein had pictures of two other great scientists on his office walls: Sir Isaac Newton and James Clerk Maxwell.

Toward the end of Einstein's life, however, he was said to have taken down the pictures of Newton and Maxwell and replaced them with two others: Mahatma Gandhi and Albert Schweitzer, a couple of great humanitarians. Someone asked him about the switch, and he replied that he had discovered it was service—and not science—that makes the difference in life. As he put it, "Only a life lived for others is a life worthwhile."

Imagine that. The man considered the greatest scientist of the twentieth century knew that science had to take a back seat when it came to doing things for other people. It's a basic truth about life, but it's one we so easily forget.

The Bible, however, won't let us forget it completely. As a follower of Christ, serving isn't really an option. It's essential. If we are ever to live life with a capital L, we have to understand that true joy and fulfillment come only when we give out what we take in, and pass on to others what we have received.

I have a friend who likes to compare it to having your arms full of Christmas presents. You can't accept any more until you've given away what you're already holding. And that's just like God's gifts and blessings. He has more he wants to give us, but we've got to make room first by offering what we already have.

Now, I'm not just talking about material things. I'm talking about giving of yourself, your time, and your talents, just for the joy of knowing it was what you were created to do. You can work at a job and be paid for it, but that will never satisfy you like finding yourself in what God wants you to do and losing yourself in his service. That's the greatest pay you'll ever receive.

special assignment

One of my grandchildren has a little toy box with different shaped holes in it. One's a triangle, one's a star, one's a circle, and one's a square. You can't put the star in the square hole, and the circle won't fit in the triangle hole. Each piece has a specific shape, and kids learn those shapes by matching the pieces with the holes they fit into.

God made each of us that way, as well. The church is full of different niches and holes, and he's created somebody specific to fill each and every one of them. In other words, there's a hole that God has for you to fill. Once you discover what it is, you'll find that everything else falls into place behind it. Let's focus on this: You and I don't just pick out a place to serve. We don't just decide, "Oh, this looks pretty interesting," and sign up. Rather, God calls us to a specific place to serve and puts his stamp of approval on it.

Consider Exodus 3:10, where God told Moses that he had chosen him to go to Pharaoh to demand the release of the captive Israelites. Moses responded, "But who am I to appear before Pharaoh? How can you expect me to lead the Israelites out of Egypt?" God responded simply, "I will be with you."

May you live all the days of your life.

—**Irish blessing, also attributed to Jonathan Swift**

That's how God works. He has things he wants us to do and places he wants us to serve, but it's not really about us. It's about him working through us to accomplish his plans. When we understand that, fulfillment comes, because we become part of a larger picture, a greater role. We start to see how our little piece fits into the grand puzzle of life.

I know of a young man who works with college students. Recently, he's been feeling called to go to China. Don't misunderstand. He doesn't want to go to China. He's been there before, and suffered some tremendous persecution at that time. But he feels drawn to the country. You know why? The ratio of non-Christians to Christians is a lot higher in China. He gets the big picture and how he fits into it.

What about you? Maybe you feel drawn to sing in the choir or to teach Sunday school. Maybe you feel led to visit people in prisons or to be an usher in the parking lot. I don't know where you're supposed to serve, but I do know this: God has a place for every person. And when he gets them there, he empowers them to do what he needs done.

God's instrument

Look at Acts 3:1–11. Peter and John were on their way to the Temple to pray. They came across a lame man who had never been able to walk. When they passed by, he begged them for money.

Peter responded: "I don't have any money for you. But I'll give you what I have. In the name of Jesus Christ of Nazareth, get up and walk!" Then Peter took him by the hand and helped him up, and the man's feet and ankles instantly became strong. He jumped to his feet and walked, and as you can imagine, all the people around him were amazed.

When Peter saw the crowds, he said, "Men of Israel, why does this surprise you? Why do you stare at us as if by our own power or godliness we had made this man walk?" Not only did Peter know that he and John had been at the right place at the right time to be used for God's service; he also knew that it really wasn't about him at all. It was simply about being willing to serve and allowing God to work through him. When God funnels his power into a particular place where he wants you to serve, miraculous things can take place.

Recall that in John 15:5, Jesus said, "I am the vine; you are the branches." All you have to do is stay connected to him, and then, it says you will "bear much fruit." God doesn't call us to be successful, or to figure it all out on our own. He just calls us to be faithful and obedient to him, and he does the rest.

making do

To be faithful on our side, we need to give our best effort at whatever we put our hands to. We find a great example to follow in Mark 14:1–9. A woman came to Jesus with some expensive perfume. She broke the bottle and began to pour it on Jesus' head as a sign of worship and devotion. Some of the others there became indignant. They rebuked her, saying that she could have sold the bottle of perfume instead and given the money to the poor.

Jesus, however, told them to leave her alone. He called her act "beautiful," and said, "She did what she could." The woman hadn't gone to the bargain basement to buy perfume. She didn't go to the place that was second rate. The Bible indicates that it was the most expensive, the best that could be bought, and Jesus was so impressed with her selflessness that he said, "Wherever the Good News is preached throughout the world, this woman's deed will be talked about in her memory." Wouldn't you like to impress Jesus like that? The way to do so is to do the best we can. Whatever we offer him should be a thing of excellence. Anything less just isn't enough.

> Use what talents you possess;
> the woods would be very silent
> if no birds sang except
> those that sang best.
>
> **—Henry van Dyke**

During World War II, a group of French soldiers was captured. They were made to work for the Germans in their munitions factory. They literally had to make bombs, knowing that some of those bombs would be dropped on their own people, possibly even their own families.

One of the captives happened to be a scientist. He figured out a way to construct the bombs so that they wouldn't actually detonate when they hit. He taught the other soldiers to make them that way. Well, the bombing started in France, but when these bombs came down, sure enough, they wouldn't explode. Experts were called in to find out what was going on, and when they disassembled one of the non-detonating bombs, there was a note inside. It said something like this: "Doing the best we can, with what we have, where we are."

And that—doing the best we can, with what we have, where we are—is the biblical standard of serving. It tells God that

we're serious about our place in his Kingdom, and that we're
serious about him, too.

eternal rewards

There's one more thing about serving God that simply
must be mentioned: It carries eternal rewards. What we do
in this life to serve Christ isn't just something we do for this
life. It's something we do for eternity. In Matthew 6:19–21,
Jesus said:

> Don't store up treasures here on earth, where they can be
> eaten by moths and get rusty, and where thieves break in
> and steal. Store your treasures in heaven, where they will
> never become moth-eaten or rusty and where they will be
> safe from thieves.

In other words, the things we store up in heaven—the
things that we do with eternal purposes in mind—are kept in
a safe place.

> We should all be concerned
> about the future because
> we will have to spend
> the rest of our lives there.
>
> —Charles F. Kettering

All the time we spend trying to gain temporal things—the
cars, the houses, the clothes—pales in comparison to the time
we spend serving in God's Kingdom. Because all those things
ultimately depreciate, but the time we invest for God multiplies
and multiplies and multiplies.

Ultimately, only the things that are done for Christ last. So
where is God leading you? Where has he tugged on your

sleeve to serve? You'll never know the joys that will come with being the right shape in the right hole at the right time until you're there.

dive in

- *What might prevent me from spending more time serving others?*
- *How could my life be enriched through service?*
- *In what areas has God given me talents and abilities that I could use for his kingdom?*

Nobody can do everything,
but everyone can do something.
—Author Unknown

chapter 31

opportunities abound

E verywhere you look, there's bound to be a need: children's ministry, choir, visiting shut-ins, teaching Bible studies, short-term missions, manning the book store or the help desk, and the list goes on.

To be honest, the list can sometimes be overwhelming. There are so many places to serve that it's possible to go one of two ways: You can either be so overcome by all the choices that you end up doing nothing at all, or you try to do so many that you end up burning yourself out. I don't advocate either. All I want you to do is find the place that you fit and stick with that.

At our church, we have an "every member commitment card." It's called "every member" because every person in the church completes one. It's a "commitment" card because members are asked to prayerfully consider their choices before they sign—and to take it seriously. There are more than 250 areas of service listed on the card, including making pancake breakfasts for the men's ministry, operating a spotlight for the religious drama ministry, driving a shuttle bus, following up with new believers, delivering flowers, helping with Boy Scouts, maintaining the bulletin board, teaching English as a second language, offering financial counseling, and everything in between.

using my gifts

Different people are called to different areas. By encouraging everyone to serve, the needs of the church are met, and the needs of the individual to "fit in" are met.

Some people have been walking in certain areas of ministry for so long that they don't have to think twice about where they belong. They know what they love and they stay there. Others may have a hard time figuring out exactly how they should be serving God and their church.

The reality is that your entire life can be spent serving God. That doesn't mean that every second of every day you're doing something to specifically help the church. It means you can serve God through your attitude, your readiness to pitch in where you're needed, and your willingness to worship him by using the skills, gifts, and abilities he has given you. We're not all good at the same things. So you shouldn't assume that just because someone gets great joy or sense of purpose out of serving somewhere, it's going to be exactly the same for you. Maybe you've tried serving in a particular area, and it left you feeling frustrated, overwhelmed, or worn out. It could be you're not meant to serve in all areas; you're meant to serve only in the ones to which God has called you.

do what you love

So how do you figure out where you're "called"? Sometimes it's clear, and sometimes it's trial and error. But when you're trying to figure out the best place to plug in, there are a few things to keep in mind.

Start by investigating where the needs are. All ministry should be based on need. Look for ministries that are bearing fruit—the places where disciples are being made and lives are changed. This can happen even through ministries that may seem insignificant, like directing cars through the parking lot or maintaining the church's bulletin board. Allow yourself to be surprised by God.

> ## To love what you do and feel that it matters—how could anything be more fun?
> **—Katherine Graham**

Find out about the ministries in your church, and see where the holes are. Discover what kind of help people in those particular areas of service are praying for, and see if those needs match up with any of your own skills or abilities. If you're good at organizing, for example, there may be a spot for you in the church office. If you like doing arts and crafts, there could be a place to serve in the children's ministry.

Maybe you have an idea that hasn't been considered. If so, great! Talk to your pastor or leadership team about how to develop that ministry. You might even find that there are others interested in the same kind of service. Your experience and ability may allow you to serve God in ways that you couldn't have even imagined.

While you're searching for the best place to get involved, ask yourself: *What am I most passionate about? What gets me the most excited, brings me the greatest joy and sense of fulfillment, and gives me a reason to get out of bed in the morning?* The answers might give you an idea of where you can serve.

Think about it this way: If you've got kids, you know what makes them the happiest. I'm not just talking about going out for ice cream or getting a present. I mean things that satisfy your children on a deeper level. Maybe you have one who likes to read and another who likes playing sports. Chances are, you're going to do whatever you can to help them grow in those areas and take part in experiencing them whenever possible, because you want them to be happy. It's the same with God. He wants us to be happy, too, and his desire is for us to live a life more satisfying than we can even imagine. He made you, he developed those passions in you, and he can help you see them fulfilled.

If you enjoy doing something, you're much more likely to do it well and with enthusiasm. When that happens in an area of service, it becomes less drudgery and more an opportunity for joy.

What would your church would be like if everyone served in a place that they enjoyed, all the needs were met, and people felt worthwhile and important? It can happen. There's an additional benefit, too. People who are rowing the boat don't have the time or interest to rock it. A church in which everyone puts skills, abilities, and talents to service is a happier church overall.

don't be afraid

It's important to say, as well, that God can put you in places of service that you never would have put yourself. That's because they might offer you a place for true growth. If we think we can handle something all on our own, there's not much room for God to work. So if you find yourself with a little bit of skill in a certain area, but you're still not sure you can pull it off, let God show you how he can be glorified through your weakness. He can make up the difference.

In addition to asking questions of your fellow church members, your leadership, and yourself, ask God where he wants you to serve. Ask him to show you the open doors in the places he wants you to be. He has a plan, and he'll let you know what it is if you're willing to ask. Then look for signs. Look for coincidences that start lining up. Listen to what the people say around you. And keep your eyes open for opportunities that pop up out of nowhere.

> ## Never let the fear of striking out get in your way.
> ### —Babe Ruth

There's something else I'd like to say about choosing your area of service. Once you have an idea of where you can be used, be serious about your commitment. Volunteering at church is not like working at a job in that you probably won't be punching a time clock. All the same, if you say you'll do something, you're not just promising the person you're speaking to; you're also promising God. Being a real servant means not taking commitment haphazardly. This is your life, and this is the ministry that God has given to you. So whatever you do, it's important to do it with all of your heart.

So, what happens if you enter a certain area of service and then find out it's not for you? There are several things to keep in mind. You've got to consider why it's not a good fit. If it's uncomfortable, ask yourself—and God—if there's a lesson to be learned in sticking it out. If you don't think that's the case, however, I'd encourage you to exit as gracefully as you can. Talk to the person in charge of that ministry, and be up front. Be willing to discuss your concerns, and you might find that another part of the same ministry is more closely aligned with your skills and abilities. In addition, if you've made specific commitments, do your best to carry them out until you can cleanly step aside. Suddenly removing yourself from an area of ministry doesn't help anyone and might do more harm than you realize. Others will be left to pick up the pieces, and you may cast doubt about whether you can be counted on in the future. Again, be up front and handle the situation with integrity.

practical matters

There's another challenge that you might face when you want to get involved in a certain area. Maybe you've volunteered for a particular act or position, and the person in charge has yet to contact you about it. Don't take it personally. If you really believe that you're supposed to be involved, volunteer again. The amount of time it takes someone to respond probably has nothing at all to do with you. Extend grace and offer the benefit of the doubt. If it's where you're supposed to be, it will happen.

When we take a step toward service on this earth, there's no telling what will follow. One thing, however, is certain: God has already prepared us for it. He did so while we weren't looking, through all the days of our life, our experiences, our abilities, our gifts, and our passions.

So go on. Give it a shot. Step out and try something—no matter what it is—and see what happens. If it's not a good fit, you'll know soon enough. Show God you're willing to serve, and he'll help you find the perfect place to do it.

dive in

- *What stands between me and the ability to give 100 percent in service to God?*
- *How have I been blessed by someone else's service to me?*
- *Are there any places that I've let pain get the best of me that could still be turned around to help someone else?*

chapter 32

team spirit

I'm a sports fan, and I like to use to sports analogies in my sermons. There are several reasons for that. First of all, sports are something that we, as a modern culture, understand. We get the idea of winners and losers, rivalries, and doing whatever it takes to be on top.

We also understand being part of something larger than ourselves. When you're in a stadium with thousands of people, all rooting for the same team, well, there's not much else like it. It provides a sense of belonging and sharing common goals.

But we also get the idea of teamwork, which plays out so beautifully in sports. Now, sports does have individual events, but for the most part, it takes a team of people—a team of committed, focused people—to pull off a win. And that philosophy goes hand in hand with our lives as Christians. It takes every single one of us, as members of God's team, to accomplish his will.

It's not just a matter of showing up, though. It's also a matter of being enthusiastic about the parts we play. Think about the winning teams you've seen in the past. One of the things those teams have in common is that they're passionate about reaching their goals—about dunking that basket, making that touchdown, or hitting that home run. And they're passionate about doing it together. These are the folks who understand that old saying that there's no "I" in "team."

If we, as members of God's team, are going to be successful in bringing other people to know God and in accomplishing his works here on earth, we need to pick up a few habits from those winning sports teams. I don't mean we'll have to learn any new end-zone dances, but I do mean that we'll have to give our all for the common good. We'll have to learn to serve others—and serve God—enthusiastically.

team uniform

First of all, consider how you identify a winning team. It should be easy enough to do, because they're the ones proudly wearing their uniforms. We, too, have uniforms, though not quite in the same way.

It is literally true that you can
succeed best and quickest by
helping others to succeed.

—Napoleon Hill

Look at Acts 2:41. Peter had just finished addressing a crowd, having explained to them that God was a God of miracles, and that Jesus, the one they had crucified, was God's son. The people, realizing what they had done, were said to be "convicted deeply," so they asked Peter what they should do. Peter responded that they should repent of their wrongdoings and be baptized, allowing them to be cleansed of their sins. So they did. And they joined the church, too—all three thousand of them. In other words, they put on their uniforms and stepped up to the plate.

Today, we proudly wear our Christian uniforms by being willing to admit that it was Christ who saved us and set us free, and by being willing to pour ourselves out in service in his name. When we allow God to give us his joy, we have extra that we can pass on to others. When we're willing to serve with no regard for our own reward, it instantly identifies us as members of a team that's markedly different from the world's me-first mentality.

support system

Second, winning teams are set apart because they're willing to help each other. The individual members are willing to step back and let someone else with greater skills and abilities step forward to accomplish the task. Think about volleyball, for example. You might think that the person who spikes the ball over the net to make a point is the most important player. Before that can happen, though, the ball is in the hands of the setter, whose job is to get the ball up in the air so the shot can be made. The task is so important that volleyball teams use hand signals to make sure the setter puts the ball in just the right spot. It's also said that setting the ball is one of the easiest things to do, but the hardest to master. Isn't that the truth when it comes to any kind of position in which we set someone else up to take the glory?

Winning teams understand that they must encourage and support one another. It's the same way for us. Consider Hebrews 10:24–25: "Think of ways to encourage one another to outbursts of love and good deeds." There's also Galatians 6:2, which says, "Share each other's troubles and problems, and in this way obey the law of Christ." In 2 Corinthians 1:3–4, we're told that the "God of all mercies" comforts us in all our troubles, so that we can comfort others. We, then, can serve others by encouraging them, supporting them, comforting them, and just being there for them in general.

accountability and authority

We can also serve by holding each other accountable. From the outside, accountability may seem like a strange thing. It can be difficult to understand why anyone would share their deepest concerns, failures, or bad habits with anyone else. But there's a freedom that comes in knowing that you're not alone—that there's someone in your life who knows the struggles you're facing. There's also a lot to be said for a good friend who's willing to speak a hard truth that you might not be able to see for yourself, just to help keep you out of trouble. Proverbs 12:1 puts it rather bluntly: "To learn, you must love discipline. It is stupid to hate correction."

Of course, correction doesn't just come from other team players. It also comes from the coach. Winning team members fully understand that the coach has their best interests at heart, so they listen.

The same holds true in our Christian walk. Not only should we be willing to listen to God, the ultimate coach, it's also a good idea for us to listen to our leaders. Hebrews 13:17 says simply, "Obey your spiritual leaders and do what they say. Their work is to watch over your souls and they know they are accountable to God. Give them reason to do this joyfully and not with sorrow."

If you've ever been in any kind of leadership position, no matter how many people you were responsible for overseeing, you've seen how this works. When everyone does what you ask them to, pulling their weight and contributing to the overall effort without complaining, everything runs a whole lot more smoothly. There are a couple of things that can spread like wildfire within a team: grumbling and enthusiasm. And when we're part of a team, we've got to carefully consider which one people will catch from us.

Following a leader's authority isn't really about how effective you think a leader is. Romans 13:1–2 says:

> Obey the government, for God is the one who put it there. All governments have been placed in power by God. So those who refuse to obey the laws of the land are refusing to obey God, and punishment will follow.

So if you're placed under a coach that you have issues with, be careful. If you disagree with some things, pray that God would either change what you don't like or change your attitude toward it. But if God has, indeed, made you part of that team, he has also placed you under the authority of the one who leads it.

common goals

Those who take part in winning teams know it's not all about them anyway. It's about the common good. There's really no room for selfishness in a team that's hitting the mark.

One of the greatest football teams of all time was at Notre Dame, back when Knute Rockne was coaching. They had a backfield called the "Four Horsemen." All four of those players made All-American. They played for four years and only lost two games. You talk about a winning team? That's a pretty good record.

> **Being part of success is more important than being personally indispensable.**
>
> **—Pat Riley**

During their senior year, these guys were undefeated and getting lots of attention, and they felt pretty good about that. So Knute Rockne decided to teach them a little lesson. He pulled out the first string line and put in the third string line. In other words, the people that he put in the game weren't nearly as good at blocking the opposing team as the players he'd taken out.

So when the Four Horsemen started to run and do what they normally did, they got stopped. They lost yardage, and lost yardage, and lost yardage. When they came off the field, Knute Rockne looked at them and said, "The Four Horsemen aren't so good without the Seven Mules up front, are they?" Without the lesser-known Seven Mules up front, clearing the way, the Four Horsemen couldn't do their job.

Now, it doesn't matter if you're a mule or a horseman. It doesn't matter if you're the quarterback or the guard or the tackle or the wide receiver. What does matter is that you're part of the team, and that everybody on the team needs everybody else to play their part.

In Philippians 2:2, Paul urged Christians to make his joy complete "by agreeing wholeheartedly with each other, loving one another, and working together with one heart and purpose. In the next verse, he continued:

> Don't be selfish; don't live to make a good impression on others. Be humble, thinking of others as better than yourself. Don't think only about your own affairs, but be interested in others, too, and what they are doing.

dependability

When you're involved in an area of ministry, serving in some way, you may think that the little part you do doesn't really matter. What difference does it make, for example, if you decide to stop serving in the nursery? You're just one person in the whole congregation, after all. If you step out, surely someone else will step in. But that misses the point. If you leave a hole somewhere, someone else filling that gap will leave a hole somewhere else, and so on, and so on.

As members of a winning team, we need to know that we can rely on each other. We need to know that everybody will show up for practice, so we'll all be ready for game time. That's the only way, when the win comes, that everyone can join in the victory.

dive in

- *What's my attitude toward serving?*
- *Am I more likely to spread a positive or negative attitude among my team?*
- *In what ways could I be a better team player?*

The true meaning of life is to plant trees, under whose shade
you do not expect to sit.

—Nelson Henderson

chapter 33

a servant's heart

group of people were discussing their churches not so
long ago, and one of the people in our congregation was
part of the bunch. Apparently, people judge the size of a
church by the number of ministers it has, so they were comparing
notes. One church had two. Another had three, and still another,
four. Then they asked the man from our church how many ministers his church had. Without hesitation, he said, "A little over
seven thousand." He hit the nail on the head—at our church,
every member is a minister. Every person is called to serve.

Many years ago, the church went through the Protestant
Reformation. This happened because the clergy had created a
gulf between themselves and the regular members of the
church, the laity. The laity were not allowed to do anything
themselves, not even read the Bible. In fact, sometimes the
priesthood would even take communion for the laity.

Along came Martin Luther and the Protestant Reformation.
When all was said and done, it eliminated that gulf between the

professional clergy and the laity, and announced that the people had equal access to God. The concept was known as the priesthood of all believers.

In the last fifty years or so, however, we've managed to recreate that gulf. Churches have grown and professional staff has been hired. With that has come a mindset that, "If we need something done, we should hire someone to do it." Of course, we can find people who will do things for money. But how much better off would we all be if we could share the load unselfishly?

The only ones among you who will be truly happy are those who have sought and found how to serve.

—Albert Schweitzer

When I talked about service earlier, I briefly touched on the difference between those volunteering to serve and those being recruited to serve. I also talked about Jesus as a volunteer servant, one willing to do whatever it took—including giving his own life—to get the job done. But how often do we, as members of the modern church, find ourselves asking, "What's in it for me?" How often do we say—or hear other people say, "I just want to come to church and be fed?"

What would happen if you sat down at lunch today and said, "Feed me," to whomever would listen? Let's say someone does, and you sit there all afternoon eating. Evening comes, and you still sit there, eating away. And into the night, as well as the next morning. You know what would happen before long? First, you'd get fat and lazy. Second, you'd be dead. You'd just stuff yourself until you couldn't take any more, and eventually, your body would not be able to stand up under the load.

Of course, it's not supposed to work that way. We're supposed to come to the table for meals periodically, and then expend that energy through work and service and other activities. The best way to stay in good shape, experts will tell you, is to make sure you're not taking in a whole lot more than you're giving out.

serving is our purpose

It works the same way with the church. The way we stay in good shape is by making sure that there's regular feeding, and that there's also regular expenditure of what we're learning and what we're experiencing. We're filled up so we can give to others out of the overflow.

When we serve others because we want to and not because we have to, it's a whole different dynamic. It changes the way we see the people we serve. It also changes the way we relate to the people in our church leadership. When that leadership has to go out and recruit people to get tasks done, they end up being tempted to be overly persuasive. If I'm a church staff member and I need a teacher for a certain class, I'm going to do everything I can to persuade you to let me recruit you. We've learned how to put the fear of God in you, you know. Let's say we need a teacher for a group of fourth graders. The pastor can come to you and make you feel guilty. He can say, "We need you to teach, and if you don't, these kids are probably going to end up in prison some day." And you won't want to say no to your pastor, so you end up doing it for the wrong reasons.

When that happens, nobody wins. That's just arm twisting, plain and simple. We might not twist those arms physically, but we sure are emotionally and intellectually. That wasn't how Jesus got things done, though. When he wanted to teach something, he didn't twist arms. Instead, he bent his knee. Look at John 13:1–15. It was near the end of Jesus' ministry on earth, and James and John had already tried to position themselves by asking who would be next to Jesus in heaven.

In the meantime, Jesus took a basin and towel, and he overcame the arguments of who would be the greatest by getting on his knees and washing the disciples' feet. At that moment, he gave them—and us—a lesson: You and I were created for a purpose, and that purpose is to serve. His Word says that if we want to be happy and fulfilled, we'll never get there just by receiving. We also have to give.

motivation

If we're going to give like Jesus did, love has to be our motivating factor.

I heard of a seventy-five-year-old woman who had been a smoker for sixty years. She'd tried everything to quit—therapy, medication, all sorts of things—but nothing could help her stop. Then she met a man and fell in love. He told her, "I can't stand smoking. If you'll quit, I'll marry you." So she quit that very day. She said that she completely lost the desire to smoke.

Love can do tremendous things, and it's so much better than a motivation of fear. Fear and intimidation might get us to do something for a little while, but rarely will it last. Sooner or later, we'll decide we've had enough.

A man was walking through a cemetery one night while taking a shortcut home, and he fell into a newly dug grave that he didn't even know was there. He tried and tried to get out, but couldn't make it. So he sat himself in a dark corner and resigned to wait until sunrise, hoping someone would find him.

It didn't take that long. Within an hour, another man walking through the cemetery fell into that same grave. He was struggling and climbing, doing whatever he could to get out. After a few minutes, the guy in the dark corner said, "You can't get out of here." But the second guy sure did!

It's all about the motivation.

lean on God

When it comes to serving others, though, I'll let you in on a secret. The best servers are not those who are the most talented, gifted, or trained. All of these qualities are important, but the real productivity comes through connection with God. When we are willing to get beyond ourselves and into his strength and abilities, that's when God's love flows through us and touches the lives of other people.

The church can't train you well enough. You can't be educated. Nobody has everything they need to do it all themselves. But through connecting with God, we can do anything. Thinking otherwise—avoiding places of service because we don't think we're good enough or qualified enough or skilled enough or whatever—is not a mark of humility. Instead, it can be a mark of pride, because what we're really saying is that we know better than God what we're capable of, whether he's helping us or not. The humble heart, on the other hand, is the one that says, "Lord, I can't do this alone, but I know that you can make up the difference."

> If you can't feed a hundred people,
> then feed just one.
>
> **—Mother Teresa**

When it comes down to it, that's really what makes the difference between the people within the church and the people outside of it: It's a matter of who we depend on. Are we depending on ourselves or depending on God?

When the world looks at the church, they should see something different. They should see something that's so different from their own way of doing things, in fact, that they're compelled to ask what causes that difference to happen. The ability to live an unselfish life, to really be able to pour yourself out in service to others, makes people sit up and take notice.

use what you have

The way I see it, the world is waiting for the church to show them what we're made of. They're waiting to see folks who will really get in there and serve. But we can be so busy saying, "If I only had this, or I only had that," that we miss it all together.

One evening, a guy was out with his girlfriend, and the moon was glistening, and he was in a romantic kind of mood. He looked into her eyes and said, "Susan, if I had a thousand arms, they'd all be around you. If I had a thousand eyes, they'd all be gazing into yours. If I had a thousand lips, they would all be kissing you." And she said, "Bill, quit complaining about what you don't have, and use what you do have!"

Are we using what we do have? Are we willing to step out there and let God pick up the slack? Amazing things can happen, you know.

There was a successful businessman in Atlanta who received a call from a friend of his at the Boys' Club, asking for a favor. A boy in the group had leukemia, but there was nobody to drive him to the hospital for treatment. Jack, the businessman, had a lot to do, but he reluctantly agreed. He got the address and drove to a dilapidated apartment downtown in a part of Atlanta where he'd never been.

When Jack went to the door, he met the boy's mother, and then followed her inside to meet Joey. The boy was so weak that he couldn't even walk, so Jack carried him out to the car. The boy's mother sat on the passenger side, and Joey laid down on the seat with his head in his mother's lap and his feet in Jack's lap. Jack, who really didn't want to be doing this, was a little irritated, but he let it slide.

As they began to drive, Jack said to the boy, "I bet you like baseball." But the boy didn't say a word. He tried again. "I bet you like basketball." Still, no answer.

A little while later, when the car stopped at a red light, the boy simply said, "Mister." Jack turned and looked at the kid, and their eyes locked. The boy asked, "Mister, are you God?" Jack didn't know what to say, so he asked, "What do you mean?"

The boy said, "Well, yesterday Mama prayed and then she told me that God was going to come and take me home. Then you came to get me. Are you God?"

And Jack said, "No, I'm not. But I'm going to be."

Joey went to the hospital, where he stayed a short time before he went home to be with Jesus. The successful businessman decided he wanted to be God's hands and feet on

> ## If you do not give, you haven't got.
> ### —E. Stanley Jones

earth, helping people. So Jack quit his job, and now works in full-time ministry.

There's no telling what God can do with us and through us when we're willing to step out. So where's God calling you to be? Where's God calling you to serve? I can promise you, you'll never make enough money, and you'll never get enough accolades in society, to make you happy. True happiness only comes through a life lived unselfishly for others. As Jesus says in John 13:14–17:

> And since I, the Lord and Teacher, have washed your feet, you ought to wash each other's feet. I have given you an example to follow. Do as I have done to you. . . . You know these things—now do them! That is the path of blessing.

dive in

- *In what areas do I feel called to serve?*
- *How do I do a task that I've been recruited for differently from one I've volunteered to do?*
- *What changes might I need to make in my life to be more available to serve?*

*We must have the same concern for persons that Christ had
. . . It's our actions that speak, not what we say.*

—Harry Denman

chapter 34
pleasing God

O ne of my younger friends, a third grader, told me
about a Sunday school teacher who gave stars to the
children for coming to class, for having their Bibles,
and for bringing other children with them. This teacher held
all these stars, getting ready to give them out. But then she
dropped them on the floor.

Little silver stars went everywhere. She got down on her
hands and knees, and began picking them up with her finger-
nails. Before long, she realized that all of the children in the
class were just sitting there, watching her. So she said, "Won't
somebody give me a hand?" The kids began to applaud.

Makes sense, doesn't it? We're brought up with the idea
that to be successful, we need the world's applause. We need
to be liked. Admired. Appreciated. Nothing wrong with all
that, of course. But problems appear when those needs
become motivation.

If we try to live the so-called "good" Christian life by serving others—all the while knowing that it might make us look good in the process—we're not likely to get anywhere. We might land a trophy or two, or a pat on the back, but when we get our reward here on earth, we forfeit the one stored up for us in heaven. We have to ask ourselves, then, which is more important? Instant gratification or eternal blessings? Pleasing God or pleasing ourselves?

target audience

Jesus actually had quite a bit to say on the topic. Consider Mark 10:29–31:

> I assure you that everyone who has given up house or brothers or sisters or mother or father or children or property, for my sake and for the Good News, will receive now in return, a hundred times over, houses, brothers, sisters, mothers, children, and property—with persecutions. And in the world to come they will have eternal life. But many who seem to be important now will be the least important then, and those who are considered least here will be the greatest then.

There's also Mark 10:21: "Go and sell all you have and give the money to the poor, and you will have treasure in heaven." To take it a step further, there's Luke 6:22:

> God blesses you who are hated and excluded and mocked and cursed because you are identified with me, the Son of Man. When that happens, rejoice! Yes, leap for joy! For a great reward awaits you in heaven. And remember, the ancient prophets were also treated that way by your ancestors.

Following God is not always the most popular choice. Sometimes we're going to make other people angry. Sometimes we'll make people uncomfortable, because our willingness to reach out may cause them to question their own lack of willingness to do the same. But God calls us to do it regardless. He calls us to be like him, to live sacrificially and to put others before ourselves. That's the only way we really please him, whether or not we're pleasing the people around us.

motivating factors

In Luke 16:13–15, Jesus was talking to the Pharisees about money and telling them, "No one can serve two masters," so they couldn't possibly serve both God and money. But then he said a revealing thing: "You like to look good in public, but God knows your evil hearts. What this world honors is an abomination in the sight of God."

Even if we think we've covered our tracks when it comes to wrong motives and that nobody will know the difference, God will. As David said to God in Psalm 139:

> You have examined my heart and know everything about me.
> You know when I sit down or stand up.
> You know my every thought when far away.
> You chart the path ahead of me and tell me when to stop
>   and rest.
> Every moment you know where I am.
> You know what I am going to say even before I say it, LORD.

In other words, there's no fooling him; and there's no point in fooling ourselves, either. The question remains, then: How do we get ourselves out of the way so we really can serve God and others with a pure heart?

people pleasing

I'll admit that this has always been a problem for me, because I like to please people. I like for people to like me. That didn't seem to be an issue for the apostles. In Acts 2:12–29, we learn that they had been performing miracles and teaching about Jesus. The area officials became jealous of all the attention and devotion the apostles were receiving, so they put them in jail. In the middle of the night, an angel came and released them. As soon as they could get there, they were back on the streets, preaching and teaching some more.

Of course, when the authorities found out, they were upset. The high priest said:

> Didn't we tell you never again to teach in this man's name? Instead, you have filled all Jerusalem with your teaching about Jesus, and you intend to blame us for his death!

Do you know what Peter said in return? "We must obey God rather than human authority." Obviously, he and the other apostles didn't really care what the authorities thought.

> Whenever you have opportunity,
> do all the good you can . . .
> every one of you likewise
> "shall receive your own reward."
> —John Wesley

A group of guys named Shadrach, Meshach, and Abednego were the same way. There's a great story about them in Daniel 3:1–30. King Nebuchadnezzer had constructed a huge gold statue and commanded that everyone in his kingdom bow down and worship it. Those who chose not to obey were to be thrown into a fiery furnace. The three men refused anyway. They knew that the statue was nothing more than an idol, and that by worshiping it they would go against God's command in Exodus 20:4–5:

> Do not make idols of any kind, whether in the shape of birds or animals or fish. You must never worship or bow down to

them, for I, the Lord your God, am a jealous God who will
not share your affection with any other god!

So when the king asked why they refused to comply with his
rules, they said:

O Nebuchadnezzar, we do not need to defend ourselves
before you. If we are thrown into the blazing furnace, the
God whom we serve is able to save us. He will rescue us from
your power, Your Majesty. But even if he doesn't, Your
Majesty can be sure that we will never serve your gods or
worship the gold statue you have set up.

Remember the rest of the story? The king threw them into
the furnace. Because they were faithful, however, God met
them there. Even though they were bound and thrown into
the flames, they came out unscathed. In fact, verse 27 says:
"Not a hair on their heads was singed, and their clothing was
not scorched. They didn't even smell of smoke!"

As a result, the king was impressed. So much so that he
made another decree:

If any people, whatever their race or nation or language,
speak a word against the God of Shadrach, Meshach, and
Abednego, they will be torn limb from limb, and their houses
will be crushed into heaps of rubble. There is no other god
who can rescue like this!

In addition, he promoted Shadrach, Meshach, and Abednego to
higher positions in Babylon.

reputation

Just because we're not supposed to care what other people
think doesn't mean God doesn't care. A funny thing often
happens: When we stop worrying about our own reputation,
God takes care of our reputation for us. We start finding

ourselves in places we didn't expect, being able to affect people we didn't expect to be able to impact.

Once again, it's our humility in the process that can make all the difference.

Now, I'd like to challenge you with one more thing. Once we decide to serve in order to please God rather than to please man, we've got to remember that God deserves excellence. He deserves nothing less than our best.

give it your all

Too often, people think that since God is going to make up the difference in the places they fall short, they don't have to put 100 percent into it themselves. But that doesn't really honor God. I hope that when people volunteer to serve the church, that whatever they do, they'll do with more excellence than anything else in their lives, including the jobs they get paid for.

In 1 Kings 7, Solomon was building a Temple to honor God. The chapter goes into great lengths describing exactly how beautiful and grand it was. In verses 13–14, we learn that Solomon had hired a man name Huram, "a craftsman skilled in bronze work," to cast pillars and other items.

Now, Huram didn't just make a couple of plain pillars. Verses 15–20 tell us that the pillars were each twenty-seven feet tall and eighteen feet across, and:

> For the tops of the pillars he made capitals of molded bronze, each 7 1/2 feet tall. Each capital was decorated with seven sets of latticework and interwoven chains. He also made two rows of pomegranates that encircled the lattice-work to decorate the capitals over the pillars. The capitals on the columns inside the foyer were shaped like lilies, and they were 6 feet tall. Each capital on the two pillars had two hundred pomegranates in two rows around them, beside the rounded surface next to the latticework.

In other words, they were fancy, made with excellence. They were made to honor God. Anything less just wouldn't have been good enough.

anonymity

Of course, excellence doesn't come by accident, and neither does humility. My father always taught me that it was more blessed to give than receive. For years, he had a little sign in his office. He recently gave it to me. It says, "Whatever it takes." Really, that sums up his life.

I hope the same could be said for all of us. "Whatever it takes" says to me that we're willing to set aside whatever we think of ourselves and what other people think of us to do whatever God asks. And that's more than just a motto. It's a biblical concept. It's all set out for us in Matthew 6:1–4:

> Take care! Don't do your good deeds publicly, to be admired, because then you will lose the reward from your Father in heaven. When you give a gift to someone in need, don't shout about it as the hypocrites do—blowing trumpets in the synagogues and streets to call attention to their acts of charity! I assure you, they have received all the reward they will ever get. But when you give to someone, don't tell your left hand what your right hand is doing. Give your gifts in secret, and your Father, who knows all secrets, will reward you.

I don't know about you, but I want to do my best to hold out for God's reward. Because I know it will be much greater applause than anyone in the world can give.

dive in

- *What motivates me to serve others?*
- *What's the danger in not giving God my best?*
- *How important is the applause of others in my life?*

Any concern too small to be turned into prayer
is too small to be made into a burden.

—*Corrie ten Boom*

chapter 35

small price to pay

D o you have a romanticized notion that service will make you feel good, and make the person being served feel great? Well, sometimes that happens, but not always. I'll bet it was the same even for Jesus.

Remember the story about Jesus washing the feet of the disciples in John 13:1–20? Just imagine it; it couldn't have been all that pleasant. He knelt by their feet, their hot, smelly, dusty feet, and I'm certain the stench rose as the water hit the dirt. That dirt must have mingled into a muddy mess, and Jesus got his hands dirty.

For a modern-day example, consider the woman who answered the desperate call for help in the nursery even though she wasn't that comfortable around children and she was wearing a new dress. All went smoothly for a while until one child, who shouldn't have been in the nursery because she was feverish, became ill. Very, very ill. And that child's breakfast went everywhere—including the front of that new dress.

If we have to be honest, that's what service is like sometimes, isn't it? It's dirty, smelly, and you don't always feel great at the end of it. But that doesn't negate the fact that we're called to serve, even when it's uncomfortable, even when it's costly. Service does cost us greatly. It costs us our time. It costs us our pride. It may even cost us financially. All that, and the person we're serving may not care. The thing is, it's not really about affecting that person anyway. It's about allowing the service to affect us. When we're willing to serve others—especially those who don't appear to deserve it—we become more like Jesus.

How willing am I to put up with the unpleasant aspects of service?

imitate Christ

We serve because Jesus commanded it and modeled it daily. Beyond that, we serve because we're needed, because that's part of being a family. There aren't enough paid staff members in the world to keep a church running to its full capacity without the volunteers.

We serve because sometimes others notice and are affected by that service. Those being touched aren't necessarily those being served. Our coworkers may notice how we spend our time. Our neighbors might see how we help others. The woman at the grocery store might notice how we let the person with a couple of items go ahead of us.

Jesus chose to spend his last night on earth serving his disciples. Have you ever wondered why? Writing teachers will often tell their students to "show, don't tell." And that's what Jesus did. Rather than offering a sermon or parable, he chose to show his disciples what service was all about. He showed that it was about humbling yourself, getting down on your hands and knees, and sometimes encountering a little dirt.

How has serving someone else changed me? How would I like for it to?

a life worthwhile

When I learned how to play tennis, my first lesson was on how to serve. I was told it was the most important thing I'd learn, too. When I went on to college, I practiced my serve three hundred times a day because, as any tennis player will tell you, serving is an advantage.

I had a Sunday school teacher who said the same thing about serving in life. "I don't care what you accomplish in life," that teacher said, "you'll never find happiness unless you lose your life in service." And God backs up that teacher. If we want life and all its fullness, the Bible tells us, it only comes when we lose ourselves in serving him.

But serving isn't just an individual thing. When we unite our service together, we can literally change our cities. If enough cities are changed, our state will change, and so on, and so forth, until the world is a changed place.

In small churches, a lot of things would simply go undone without the people willing to serve. In larger churches, the service itself may not be as important as the connections it provides to those we serve with. When we work on a project together or serve on a committee, we get to know people in a way that being together for worship on Sundays doesn't allow. We develop deep friendships out of our joint experiences. We develop the kind of relationships that just don't grow easily on their own.

Am I willing to connect with others through service?

opportunities abound

You may remember Sir Isaac Newton from your high school science books. Usually, if there was a picture with the lesson, it was an illustration of Newton sitting under a tree when an apple fell on his head, giving birth to the theory of gravity. Newton had another theory, too, about inertia. Simply stated, the theory of inertia says that an object at rest will remain at rest, and an object in motion will remain in motion unless altered by some great force.

So what does that mean in regard to service? It means if you're already doing something, it's much easier for you to find and move into the right place of service than it would be otherwise. If you're doing nothing, getting started can appear to be almost impossible. You see, nature abhors a vacuum and whatever vacuums exist in your time, you'll fill with something. If you're not already serving, will an opportunity come up that will draw you away from that tennis league or the wine club or the TV show?

Even if you're not sure where you'd like to serve, or if you're not yet hearing God clearly, jump in somewhere. Test the waters by finding a place that doesn't require a long-term commitment. Serve there until you find the next place. Keep moving until you figure out the long-term picture. Otherwise, you'll be that object at rest, both inert and unserving, and you won't get anywhere at all.

Am I in motion? If not, what will it take to get me going?

team spirit

Service can be contagious when we see what we're getting out of it. And no, I don't mean serving out of pride.

We, as humans, long for a reason to exist. How many times have you heard people say they're searching for the meaning of life? Here's a little secret: The meaning of life is to be in fellowship with God and to give our lives away in service to each other. Without those two things, we'll never truly be satisfied.

We receive many other things from serving. When we serve with excellence, we reap the rewards of a job well done. When we serve with humility, we make lifelong friends, sometimes with the people with whom we serve, and sometimes with the people we serve. When we serve with enthusiasm, we can get through any service project, no matter how dirty, smelly, physically demanding, or unpleasant. As with so many things that we've talked about, our attitude can make such a difference. Remember, the condition of our hearts concerns God a lot more than our circumstances do. Are we serving enthusiastically no matter how unpleasant the task?

Am I allowing my body to be God's hands and feet on earth?

a servant's heart

Service is usually, by its very nature, an act of selflessness. Of course, we can let selfishness enter in when we're doing it for the wrong reasons, such as seeing our name in the bulletin, being seen by people we want to impress, or trying to impress God.

Since God tells us to store up treasures in heaven, what happens when we receive the rewards here on earth? If we seek recognition for our service here on earth, it's almost as if God's up in heaven marking this activity "paid in full." Do you really want to settle for your name in the bulletin rather than a treasure in heaven?

Here's a challenge for you: No matter what your motives are in the beginning, if you serve long enough, you'll usually find that selfish reasons give way to unselfish ones. You'll meet a person being helped by your service who will touch you in some way, and suddenly, you'll find a different motivation. When that happens, you'll serve more enthusiastically and with excellence because you'll see why—truly why—you're serving in the first place.

Maybe you thought it was to get your name into the bulletin or to impress the leadership. But when you see skin and bones on the results of your service, you can't help but be changed. Are you willing to let God move you from selfish reasons into unselfish ones? Are you willing to stay close to the vine so that you might bear fruit in your service?

Am I willing to delay receiving my reward until I get to heaven?

pleasing God

Could it really be so simple as this? Service done will please God. Now, our hearts may not be in the right place as we begin the process, but God will use our service to get our hearts in position so that we can truly serve unselfishly and enthusiastically.

Sometimes God needs to get us somewhere before he can begin to change our hearts.

If you find that your heart isn't ready to serve for unselfish reasons or to jump in with enthusiasm, would you be bold enough to dive in anyway? To allow God to use the very thing which you dread to change your heart towards it?

Of course, that means showing up when we say we'll be there. It means doing what's asked of us while we're serving and doing so pleasantly. There's no point in grumbling about your service while you're doing it. No point in making everyone else miserable, too. But are you willing to volunteer at your church simply because God says it's the best way?

Are you willing to do something that you are afraid to do because you believe God has called you to it? I'm not talking about performing surgery as a medical missionary when you haven't been to medical school. I'm talking about visiting shut-ins when you're not comfortable around old people or assisting in Sunday school when you don't know how to relate to children. Whatever the task, remember: God doesn't call the qualified. He qualifies the called.

Am I willing to overlook my own inabilities to follow God?

part VI

filling the bucket
to overflowing

Neither a wise man nor a brave man lies down on the tracks of history to wait for the train of the future to run over him.
—*Dwight D. Eisenhower*

chapter 36

where you're headed

I saw a great article recently about how to surf. I don't mean surfing the Web. It depicted how to actually get out in the ocean and catch a wave. You could tell that the person who wrote it, Chris Payne, had a lot of personal experience in the subject. I have to admit, the article made it sound doable. That doesn't mean it really is. I could probably follow the instructions to the letter and never get up on the board.

Between the lines, however, I saw some great wisdom about catching the wave of momentum to say afloat in this big ocean we call life. We're almost at the end of this study. How do we put into practice the things that we've learned for the long term? How do we stay up on the board, riding the waves of God's grace and provision, rather than being pulled back by the world's undertow?

firm foundation

Well, if we follow our learning-to-surf example, we begin by making sure that we've got a board. It'll be a solid foundation for our feet. In our Christian walk, that foundation starts with God's Word. Studying the Bible helps us know God better, and in the process, helps us know ourselves better, too.

Oh give me that book! . . . Let me be a man of one book.

—John Wesley

I can't tell you how many times I get calls from people who are really troubled, and they say, "John Ed, what does the Bible say about my situation? Where can I find some help?" They're basically trying to borrow somebody else's knowledge about the Bible. But the best thing is for us to be rooted and grounded in God's Word ourselves, so that his direction and guidance will come directly to us. See, we can't be casual about it.

Some folks say they just pick up their Bibles every now and then to look. Have you ever heard the story about the man who decided he'd just flip open his Bible to see what God's Word was for him that particular day? He opened it up, put his finger on a verse, and read that Judas went out and hung himself. Not sure how that applied to his own life, he thought he'd try again. This time he found a passage that said, "Do likewise." He said to himself, "Obviously there must be something wrong. God wouldn't tell me to do that." So he tried again. And finally, he flipped the page, put his finger down and read, "What thou doest, do quickly."

See what can happen when we try to just pick the Bible up here and there, rather than looking at the whole picture and studying it regularly? It'd be like trying to learn to surf while only hitting the ocean one day a year.

OK, back to our surfing analogy. Let's assume we've got that board in place—or at the very least, we're working on acquiring it. The next thing you need, if you want to learn how to surf, is something to wear. The author suggests a wet suit. You could ignore his advice, but it wouldn't be smart. Otherwise, you might end up wearing nothing if you wipe out.

Now, in the context of our surf with God, this relates to humility. Unless we're willing to humble ourselves and admit that God really does know better than we do, there's no way we're getting up on that board. The counsel of others who have gone before us is invaluable, too. Look around you at the Christian leaders in your life. I guarantee each one has something to teach you, if you're willing to learn.

persistent prayer

The surfing article also talked about leashes. Did you know that surfers use leashes to stay connected to their boards? They're usually made of plastic, and surfers attach one end to the board and another to the foot. That way, if and when they fall off, the board won't get swept away by the waves. In the same way, we stay connected through prayer. As Christians, prayer isn't just something we talk about doing, it's something we actually do. It's something that we feel deep in our hearts, something that offers us peace, direction, joy, and inexhaustible power. But it's not a one-shot deal; it's persistence.

I read an article in the paper about a seventy-four-year-old man who got married for the first time. His bride was seventy-four, too. When they were teenagers, they dated each other and had become engaged. They had a lover's quarrel, however, and split. The man never gave up, and they ended up moving into apartment houses right next to each other. For forty-two years, he regularly wrote letters to his sweetheart, asking for her forgiveness, and he put them under her door. She never responded.

One day, after all that time and all those letters, he decided not to put a letter under the door, but to knock instead. When he did, she came to the door. He said, "I'm sorry. Would you forgive me?" She said, "I will." He said, "Will you marry me?" and she said, "I will."

Have we ever been that persistent about anything? How patient are we when it comes to waiting on God?

buddy system

There's something else I found interesting in that surfing article. It said that the most important thing to have when learning to surf was someone to surf with. I like this: not only will it cut your chances of being eaten by a shark in half, the article said, but that person can also give you moral support, keep you stoked when you get frustrated, and encourage you to go for it when the waves are big.

Once again, that's so important in the faith. When we surround ourselves with other Christians and remind each other that we're all in this together, we learn so much more. We find ourselves being more willing to step out and take risks, knowing that we're never alone.

The surfing article also says you'll need some wax and some sunblock. You can make up your own connections there. But there's one more tip that's especially relevant. "When trying to stand up, stand up," the surfer wrote. "Don't get to your knees first; that leads to kneeboarding."

determine your destination

We have to decide how seriously we're going to take all of this, and whether we're going to have the courage to stand up and do it right. We always have a choice of which direction to go.

My grandchildren love the story of *Through the Looking Glass*. If you remember, Alice wasn't sure which way she should go, so she asked the Cheshire Cat for advice. "Would you tell me, please, which way I ought to go from here?"

The cat responded, "That depends a good deal on where you want to go."

"I don't much care where—" said Alice.

"Then it doesn't matter which way you go," said the cat.

"—so long as I get somewhere," Alice added as explanation.

"Oh, you're sure to do that," said the cat, "if you only walk long enough."

So the question I'm asking is, when you get where you're going, where will you be? Every so often, it's important for us to step back and ask, *Where is this path I'm taking headed? Where will I be a year from now? Five years from now? Twenty-five years from now?*

> The Christian is not one who has gone all the way with Christ. None of us has. The Christian is one who has found the right road.
>
> **—Charles L. Allen**

Jesus was pretty clear that there are only two paths we can follow: one that leads to destruction, and another that leads to life. In Psalm 119:35, David said that his happiness was found along the path of God's commands. It can be the same for us, but it's going to take some sense of intent and purpose.

Jesus, of course, provides us a great example. When faced with the decision of continuing on to Jerusalem, where he would surely face his death, Luke 9:51 tells us that he had "resolved" to go. Other translations say he "steadfastly set his face." He was focused and certain. He knew that by taking that road, it would fulfill his purpose on earth.

In other words, he wouldn't have been satisfied by just kneeling on the board, rather than standing. That would have been the wrong way to get to where he needed to go.

So often, we think we're just going to stumble upon God's plan for our lives, that we're going to catch the great wave that carries us all the way to shore just by happenstance. It doesn't work that way. Like Jesus, we need intent and purpose. Sure, we can catch one wave or another. We can choose our path, and eventually, we'll end up somewhere. But wrong roads rarely lead to right places.

The thing is, we're held accountable for what we've been taught. As it says in James 4:17, "It is sin to know what you ought to do and then not to do it." In other words, if you've received any new understanding or revelation recently, you'll now be held accountable for that, too. When you come before the judgment seat of God, you won't be able to say, "I didn't know." On the other hand, the good news is that when we know the right thing to do, we can set about doing it.

If you don't know where you're going, every road will get you nowhere.
—Henry Kissinger

In 2 Timothy 4, Paul was looking back over the years. He knew that he was near death, and was thankful that his life had "already been poured out as an offering to God." In verses 7–8, he continued:

> I have fought a good fight, I have finished the race, and I have remained faithful. And now the prize awaits me—the crown of righteousness that the Lord, the righteous Judge, will give me on that great day of his return. And the prize is not just for me but for all who eagerly look forward to his glorious return.

How great it would be if we could all look back, years from now, and know with certainty that we did the best we could. How great it would be to realize that we were willing to get in the water, strap our foot to the board, take a deep breath, and stand.

It is possible, you know. It just takes one day at a time, paying attention to where the waves take us, and being committed to choosing the right ones.

One final lesson from that article: Learning to catch the wave, it says, is a hurdle that needs to be overcome.

> The wave knowledge—knowing which wave to paddle for and which to let pass, and the timing—when to start paddling, how fast, how much to arch your back, and when to get to your feet, are things that no one can teach you.

That knowledge will only come with time spent surfing.

dive in

- *How sturdy is my board?*
- *How secure is my leash?*
- *How can I get better at recognizing the right waves to catch?*

When I was young I was sure of everything . . . at present,
I am hardly sure of anything but what God has revealed to me.
— *John Wesley*

chapter 37

spiritual maturity

I f you know anything at all about lobsters, you know that they have pretty tough shells. Their shells help protect them from danger, and you would think that, as hard as they are, they'd been there all of the lobster's life. Actually, though, lobsters grow by molting, or struggling out of their shells, as they absorb water. Water makes their body size increase, and it's said that lobsters can shed their shells twenty-five times in the first five to seven years of life as they continue to grow.

Each time that molting occurs, the new shell begins as a soft one. It takes a little while for it to harden, so during that time, the lobster is vulnerable to both disease and predators.

I believe we can be vulnerable in the same way. When we begin to grow, our old shells, or old ways of doing things, no longer fit. We then shed those shells, but when we do, we temporarily put ourselves in precarious positions. While we're in the process of finding new paths, we may leave ourselves open to predators just as the lobsters do. We risk falling back into old habits before the new ones are established.

The good news is that God continues to offer us bigger and better shells to grow into. As we find new place after new place, and watch new shell after new shell grow, we become increasingly confident that there's always more where that came from. We learn by experience that growth is a positive thing. God is in the business, after all, of making us more and more like him, so we can increasingly reflect his glory.

it takes time

Remember, though, it's going to take some time. You can't get there overnight. Look at what Paul says in Colossians 2:6–7:

> And now, just as you accepted Christ Jesus as your Lord, you must continue to live in obedience to him. Let your roots grow down into him and draw up nourishment from him, so you will grow in faith, strong and vigorous in the truth you were taught. Let your lives overflow with thanksgiving for all he has done.

When you plant a seed, you can't expect to come back the next day and find a piece of fruit. If you take the time to let the roots go into the soil, you'll eventually have a little plant. If you tend to that plant, it will eventually bear fruit. It doesn't happen right away, but it does happen.

I've got a friend who's trying to lose some weight. The toughest thing about it is that you can't lose, say, twenty pounds in one day. It takes time. In the same way, if you enroll in a college today, you're not going to receive your degree tomorrow. You can't go from being a freshman to a senior in a week. You've got to persistently complete each course, one by one, until you finally earn that degree.

discipline

Spiritual maturity is exactly the same. It not only takes time, it also takes discipline. Here's something else to take note of:

The word discipline is a lot like the word disciple. Disciples, then, are those who are disciplined.

In 1 Timothy 4:7–8, Paul says:

> Spend your time and energy in training yourself for spiritual fitness. Physical exercise has some value, but spiritual exercise is much more important, for it promises a reward in both this life and the next.

Of course, athletes put in a lot of hours and a lot of effort preparing themselves for the game. Right now, society is in the middle of a physical fitness craze. Have you noticed how many clubs, gyms, and spas exist? Doctors are increasingly telling us that we need to be physically fit. To do that, it takes discipline. I'd love to tell you that you could just sit there in your chair and magically get in shape. But you can't. You've got to be disciplined. Committed.

I've asked a couple of ex-professional football players in our congregation about how hard it was to play sports at that level. They told me that you've got to stay with it. You've got to work with those weights. You've got to run those wind sprints. You not only have to get in shape, you also have to stay there.

> **Spiritual life does not remove us from the world but leads us deeper into it.**
>
> **—Henri J. M. Nouwen**

For those of you who want to get into better shape, I've got little story for you. A man was trying to lose weight, so he went to the doctor, who said, "All right, I'm going to give you a prescription. There are two things you can't eat: sweets and bread. Beyond that, I want you to exercise."

The man returned to the doctor a few weeks later, and the doctor saw that he had lost some weight. He asked the man, "How's it going?"

And he replied, "Tough."

"But it looks like you're losing weight. Have you stayed away from sweets and bread?"

The man nodded.

"And what about exercise? What are you doing?"

He said, "I'm climbing the walls."

Funny, but true. Sometimes the very idea of being disciplined makes us crazy. But if we're ever going to get anywhere, we've got to take it seriously.

Are you disciplined in studying God's Word? Are you disciplined in prayer? Are you disciplined in serving? Are you disciplined in how you use your finances? You can't just sit back and say, "Oh, it's all going to work out." It takes a plan, it takes time, and it takes discipline.

devotion

One more thing it takes, and that's devotion. It's when we seek God with all of our heart, Deuteronomy 4:29 tells us, that we find him. Look at the words of Jesus in Luke 9:23–24:

> Then he said to the crowd, "If any of you wants to be my follower, you must put aside your selfish ambition, shoulder your cross daily, and follow me. If you try to keep your life for yourself, you will lose it. But if you give up your life for me, you will find true life."

Now that's commitment. That's when we crave God so much, we want him more than anything else in the world. That's also when we're compelled to pray, to study his Word, and to tell others about him. We can't help it, because we're motivated by love.

A pastor friend, John, has a great tale about love and how it can motivate a person. John lived in Missouri, but was being transferred to Alabama, where the woman he wanted to marry lived.

John decided it was time to marry her, so he went to a jeweler in his hometown and asked if he could see some engagement and wedding rings. The selection was narrowed down pretty quickly, according to what he could afford. There were only a couple of rings to choose from, because John had only been out of college a little while and had used up most of his savings to pay off student loans.

John explained to the jeweler that there was only one ring he really wanted, but if he bought it, it would just about clean him out. In fact, he said, it would only leave him enough money to drive to Alabama, ask her to marry him, and drive back.

John went ahead and wrote the check that cleaned him out. The reason he did it, he said, was that he had been talking to a friend about how much money he should spend on an engagement ring. The friend had asked, "Well, how much do you love the girl? You're only going to do this once, right? Put as much in it as you can. It would be the best thing you could do."

> It is in the process of being worshipped that God communicates his presence to men.
>
> —C. S. Lewis

John said that he has never regretted that advice. The ring wasn't by any means a large one, but he could take comfort in the fact that he had given her the best he could. John wanted her to know that he loved her with all he had, and that he loved her more than anyone else.

That's what God wants from us, too. He wants us to love him with all we have, and to be willing to love him more than anyone or anything else. This is where the idea of worship comes in, and it's so much more than liturgy and hymn singing, which is what some people term worship. Worshiping God means living to please him in everything we do, honoring him with our words and actions. It means trusting him and believing what he promises us in the Bible. It's having a passion to see his will accomplished and to bring other people to him.

growing up

I heard about an eighty-five-year-old man who talked about continuing to grow in Christ every day. That's where I want to be! This man said, "If I cease to grow, I'll die. So when I can run, I'm going to run. When I can walk, I'll walk. When I can only crawl, then I'll crawl. But, by the grace of God, I'll at least always be moving forward."

I hope you're always moving forward, too, instead of sliding backward; because eventually, even in spite of yourself, you will get there. You will grow.

At this point, the question may be, "How do I know when I'm there? How do I know when I'm spiritually mature?" The truth is that spiritual maturity is obvious. If you see a baby that was just born, and then you see that same baby three years later, it's obvious that something has happened. In the same way, when God is helping us grow, it's obvious.

First of all, there's the love. It becomes the motivating factor in how we deal with other people.

In Massachusetts, there's a structure known as the "I Love You" lighthouse. It was built on a rocky outcropping in the mid-1800s, and the sad story is that a heavy storm hit the tower, tearing it apart and killing two assistant keepers in the process. The tower was rebuilt, and as a tribute to those who had died, the beacon was given a unique 1-4-3 flashing sequence, just like the letters in the phrase. Everybody who sees it remembers what it means.

What if we, as Christians, went around flashing "I love you"? How could we change the world by really loving the people around us, no matter who they are? It would be a sure sign that we had allowed Jesus to touch our hearts and help us grow.

Same thing with the fruit we're producing. Love is one of the fruits of the Spirit found in Galatians 5:22–23. The others include joy, peace, patience, kindness, goodness, faithfulness, gentleness, and self-control. When the Holy Spirit controls our lives, verse 22 says, "he will produce this kind of fruit in us."

Are we seeing these things in ourselves? Are we seeing them in others? They're a good sign that we've allowed God to work in us. They're a good sign, too, that we've shed some of those old shells along the way—and there are still bigger and better ones to come.

dive in

- *On a scale of one to ten, how disciplined am I in my relationship with God?*
- *Do I do things for God out of love or obedience?*
- *What kind of shells has God helped me shed as I've learned to walk with him?*

There are many of us that are willing to do great things for the Lord, but few of us who are willing to do little things.

—Dwight L. Moody

chapter 38

sharing your faith

There's nothing quite like fishing on the lake. Some of us just do it for fun, but others make a living at it.

One of those professionals recently won a lot of money at a big tournament. When they interviewed him afterward, someone asked, "What makes you such a good fisherman? Do you study other fishermen?"

The man said, "No."

The interviewer said, "Then you must study all of the equipment that's available for you to use."

And again, the man said, "No."

The interviewer said, "Then what is it? How are you such a good fisherman?"

And the man responded, "I study the fish, and I try to go where the fish are."

Now, I don't really know that much about fishing, but that sounds like a pretty good way to do it. It doesn't matter how anybody else does it. It doesn't matter what kind of equipment's available. All you have to do is study the fish, and go where they are.

When you read about the ministry of Jesus, you find that it began in the synagogue, where he would preach and teach. People were amazed at the wisdom and insight he had. Before long, though, that ministry changed. He decided to go out where the fish were; he began to teach outside the synagogue.

fishers of men

In Luke 5:1–11, Jesus was teaching on the shores of the Sea of Galilee. People crowded around him, so much so that he turned around and stepped into a little fishing boat, pushed it out from the shore, and continued teaching from there. When he was done, he said something that most men would love to hear: go fishing. Actually, he said, "Now go out where it is deeper and let down your nets, and you will catch many fish." He didn't say, "Hey, do you guys think it would be a good idea? Do you feel like fishing today?" No, he said, "Go." It's a command. When Jesus wants something done, he picks someone out and tells that person to do it.

They pushed out and started fishing. At the end of passage, we see why he told them to do that. He helped them bring in a big catch to show that it was possible; then Jesus told them he wanted them to go fishing for people.

No matter how you feel about it, the number one task of the church today is to fish. God tells us we're supposed to go. You've heard that old adage, "Give a man a fish, feed him for a day; teach a man to fish, feed him for a lifetime." One woman said, "I discovered if I give my husband a fish, he's got a meal. But if I teach him how to fish, I can get rid of him every weekend."

Fishing can be fun. We don't have to look at it as a chore. We can chose to see it as an opportunity to partner with God in his work, a chance to grow in our faith, and a sure way to have an impact on eternity.

confidence

All the same, the whole idea can be pretty intimidating. So let's break it down and take it step by step. First of all, if you and I are going to share our faith and do so effectively, we're going to have to do it with confidence. Look at Acts 4:13. Peter and John had just finished sharing their faith with a council of elders and teachers in Jerusalem. The members of that council were amazed when they saw the boldness of Peter and John, "for they could see that they were ordinary men who had had no special training. They also recognized them as men who had been with Jesus."

No matter what you're up to, if you're not doing it with confidence, you're likely to fail. The confidence of Peter and John didn't come from any education or training. It didn't come because they trusted in themselves or their own abilities. It came because they trusted in God and what he was doing through them.

It works the same way for us. When we're sharing our faith, confidence doesn't come through learning some kind of formula. It doesn't come with excessive education and training. It comes when I realize that it's not about what I'm trying to do, but rather what God is going to do through me.

> If you hear a voice within you say "You are not a painter," then by all means paint, and that voice will be silenced . . .
>
> **—Vincent Van Gogh**

I love the story of David and Goliath in 1 Samuel 17. When little David stepped out to face him, Goliath laughed. He was nine feet tall and covered in armor, and here was a boy with nothing but a slingshot. That giant said, "Come over here, and I'll give your flesh to the birds and wild animals!" Wouldn't that make you quiver?

But little David was confident, not in what he could do but in what God had called him to do. Remember what he said to that giant? "I come to you in the name of the LORD Almighty." He also said that the battle belonged to the Lord. You see, it's God's battle, not ours. Even if the best we can do is to show up with a slingshot, he can take care of the rest.

companionship

It's not just about confidence, though. Sharing your faith is also about companionship. Remember how the council recognized that Peter and John had been with Jesus? It only makes sense that if our confidence is in his name, that he'll be with us.

Look at Matthew 28:19–20. Jesus said:

> Go and make disciples of all the nations, baptizing them in the name of the Father and the Son and the Holy Spirit. Teach these new disciples to obey all the commands I have given you. And be sure of this: I am with you always, even to the end of the age.

It's so important for us to remember that when we go out to share our faith, he goes with us. He walks beside us. The church could spend twenty-five hours a week trying to train people to share their faith, but it would never be effective without the understanding that it's done in the name of the Lord.

credibility

Another important part of the equation is credibility. At the moment Peter and John were standing before the elders, there was another person with them: a man who had been healed by Jesus. He had been lame for more than forty years, and everyone knew it. As the popular saying goes: "Seeing is believing." Their story became all the more credible because they had a living, breathing example right next to them of what Jesus had been able to do.

In our own lives, we're the living, breathing examples. We're pictures of what Jesus can do in a changed life. If we're willing to walk the walk and not just talk the talk, people see that. That's what brings credibility to whatever it is we're trying to say.

> The only man I know who behaves sensibly is my tailor; he takes my measurements anew each time he sees me. The rest go on with their old measurements and expect me to fit them.

—**George Bernard Shaw**

Do the people around you know you to be a changed person? Do they know that you're serious about your faith, and that you believe God is real? And if so, how?

A witness, by definition, is one who has seen. And one who has seen offers a great deal of credibility.

conviction

Of course, you've got to have conviction to go along with it, as well. Peter and John had that closed-minded council in such an uproar that the council told them they could never again teach or speak about Jesus. In verse 19, they responded, "Do you think God wants us to obey you rather than him? We cannot stop telling about the wonderful things we have seen and heard." They were under the conviction that they weren't there to please the people; they were there to please God.

Some time ago, the state's prison commissioner was a member of this church. What a man of conviction. He always said that the way to get prison reform was to change people's hearts. It doesn't matter how long people are behind bars before they get out. It matters if their hearts have been changed.

That man helped open up our state's correction facilities to prison ministry, and I'll never forget one night when he spoke in our fellowship hall. Chuck Colson and Bill Glass, a couple of prison ministry visionaries, had come to share with our congregation. They asked the commissioner if he had anything to say.

As I remember it, he reached into his billfold, took out a piece of paper, and said that it contained the names of three people who had been executed since he had been commissioner of corrections. He said, "and for each of them, just before they were executed, the man pulling the switch looked at me because I had to give the final nod."

He carried those names with him every day, he said, and often wondered: Didn't they know somebody who was a Christian? Didn't they work for somebody who was a Christian? Didn't they have a Sunday school class that cared for them? Didn't they have a neighbor? Those names reminded him, he said, that people can totally escape the faith witness of anybody.

Never believe that a few caring people can't change the world. For indeed, that's all who ever have.

—Margaret Mead

How many people do we come in contact with during a typical day? How much of a conviction do we feel to make sure they don't escape the witness, too? Are we like Peter and John who "cannot stop telling about the wonderful things" they'd seen and heard?

communication

The next piece to the puzzle is communication. Peter and John weren't just talking. They were sharing their faith out of love, so it came across as winsome and inviting.

The other day, I heard about a company that wanted to change its health insurance. One of the prerequisites, though, was that every employee had to sign on. Well, everybody did except for one man. He just refused. His supervisors talked to him about it, but he still refused. So they went to the president of the company and told him what was happening, and the president said he'd take care of it.

The president called the man into his office, and he said, "They tell me you don't want to sign up for this insurance policy with the rest of us." And the man said, "That's right." The president asked, "Can you give me a good reason why?" The man said, "I just don't want to." The president said, "Well, let me explain it to you this way. If you don't sign up for it, you're fired."

When that man came out of the president's office, everybody was watching. He said, "Well, I signed up. We're ready to go." Someone asked him, "What made you change your mind?" And he said, "See that man sitting in that office? He explained it to me in terms that I could understand."

If we're going to be effective, good communication is key. We need to make sure that we do our best to explain things in terms people understand. That's the only way they'll get it. The truth is, sometimes we do a pathetic job when it comes to sharing our faith. We use words people don't know, and try to make things more difficult than they really are. People often ask, "Can't I just communicate with my actions?" Well, no. It takes both actions and words, and a real love for the person we're trying to reach.

When God's the one who's providing that love, though, there's a great result. Our family starts to grow. Sharing that love with others really doesn't have to be a burden. All it takes is a little confidence, companionship, credibility, conviction, and communication—and a willingness to drop our nets and see what we can catch.

dive in

- *What holds me back from throwing out my net?*
- *How can God help me be more confident about sharing my faith?*
- *With whom in my life do I need to share my faith?*

Ring the bells that still can ring.
Forget your perfect offering. There is a crack in everything.
That's how the light gets in.

—*Leonard Cohen*

chapter 39

a standard of excellence

I 've been spending some time looking for the perfect quote. And I do mean "perfect," because we're about to address the difference between perfection and excellence. You see, Jesus, in his thirty-three years on this earth, lived a perfect, sinless life. In trying to be more like him, a lot of Christians misunderstand and think that they're supposed to be perfect, as well. Some of them miss the mark by so much that they get discouraged and quit trying. There's a reason, however, that they call the gospel "good news." It's good because God already knows we're not perfect. He knows we're going to fail, we're going slip up, we're going to do things that seemed right at the time, but in hindsight, weren't. And you know what? He loves us anyway.

I sometimes wonder if God is up in heaven just shaking his head at how silly we can be. I wonder what he thinks of all our lists of shoulds and shouldn'ts, and the things for which we end up judging other people. I wonder if he gets frustrated by how much time we spend worrying about other people's faults rather than working on our own.

I actually found a few quotes on perfection that I really like. First, one by an unknown author: "The most difficult part of attaining perfection is finding something to do for an encore." Once we get to perfect, there's nowhere else to go.

George Fisher said: "When you aim for perfection, you discover it's a moving target." It's always the unattainable goal, just out of reach, like the proverbial carrot on a stick, dangled in front of our noses. No matter how close we are—or, rather, how close we think we are—we never quite make it.

One more quote that really made me think is by author and journalist Anna Quindlen. She said: "The thing that is really hard, and really amazing, is giving up on being perfect and beginning the work of becoming yourself." One reason that quote is so thought-provoking is that we're faced with what Jesus said in Matthew 5:48: "Be perfect, therefore, as your Heavenly Father is perfect." How is it that Jesus can command us to be perfect, knowing full well that as long as we're on this earth, we'll never get there? Here's a thought: As Christians, God lives within us. And God is perfect in every way. As such, the bigger we allow him to be in our behaviors, our lives, our thoughts, our desires, the more perfect we become.

model of perfection

Thank goodness, God sent his son, Jesus, to earth as a role model of what perfection looks like in human form. The very reason God created us is to be like him.

There's a story about a rather wealthy Christian gentleman whose son was slightly deformed. The doctors didn't know exactly what to do for him, but said that if the father could provide him with an image that showed him the possibilities of what he could become, it might help.

So the father had a sculptor create a statue of Jesus. It had a winsome and inviting face and outstretched arms, and it stood about five feet, ten inches, the projected height of his young son.

He asked his son to look at the statue several times every day. The boy did this. Every day, in the morning, afternoon, and evening, he would look at the statue. For a while, nothing happened. But over time, there was some improvement, his little body began to straighten up. The more he saw that statue, the more he wanted to be like it. One day, he stood up straight, and he finally was like it.

> Not my responsibility,
> but my response to His ability.
>
> —E. Stanley Jones

The more we keep our eyes on Jesus, the more we want to be like him. The more we learn about his honesty, passion, wisdom, example, power, and life, the more appealing he becomes.

be yourself

At the same time, another thing happens: We begin to let go of the psychological trap of thinking we have to be perfect to be accepted by God—or anyone else, for that matter. The more we know Jesus, the more we realize that we already are accepted, and our lives become more about doing our best than being the best. It's like Quindlen said: We finally start beginning the work of becoming ourselves. Those selves eventually start to move on to perfection. In other words, they stand up straight and become like Jesus.

What does it really mean to become like Jesus? First of all, it means evaluation. It means there has to be a time that we stop and take a good look at our lives. The idea is for me to ask myself, *Where am I? Am I more like Jesus today than I was a year ago?* Are you? Are you willing to make a commitment to become more like Jesus? That's the very desire of God.

Have you seen some growth in the past month? Do the people around you see you becoming more like Jesus, growing and changing before their eyes? Are you connected to God as the source of power, or are you still trying to do things on your own? Have you seen any miracles in your life or experienced any answered prayers? Do you daily ask God to guide you, even in little things? This may seem like an exhausting list, but it's meant more as a jumping-off point to get you thinking. Don't worry; none of us has it all just right. None of us, remember, is perfect.

The best of it is, God is with us.

—John Wesley

Regular evaluation, however, a willingness to humbly ask ourselves—and ask God—where we are, can help us get there. So can recognizing what God has already done. Colossians 1:12 tells us that, as believers, we're enabled to share the inheritance that belongs to God's holy people. In other words, we're qualified, and God is the one who qualifies us. All we have to do is respond to the grace he's so freely given.

If you still don't understand that concept of grace, try this. Romans 5:6–8 says:

> When we were utterly helpless, Christ came at just the right time and died for us sinners. Now, no one is likely to die for a good person, though someone might be willing to die for a person who is especially good. But God showed his great love for us by sending Christ to die for us while we were still sinners.

It's almost too much to fathom, that Christ died for me and for you. But it's the truth.

aim for excellence

That explains a lot. It explains why, when we really get to know God, that anything less than excellence just isn't enough for him. Anything else just doesn't meet his standard. Understanding this can take a real change of heart, but fortunately, it's not a change we make on our own. It's more something that we respond to. With God's help, we can choose new life. We're promised in 2 Corinthians 5:17 that "those who become Christians become new persons. They are not the same anymore, for the old life is gone. A new life has begun!" In other words, he allows us to start over, to shed that old lobster shell. All the old things pass away. God tells us that he doesn't care what we've done in the past. It's gone and gone forever, and through Christ, he allows us to wipe that slate clean. Not just once, but time and time again. His love for us knows no limits, and if we'll allow it, that love can seep into every pore of our being.

Sometimes, though, we can get frustrated because we think we're supposed to earn that love and that grace, and we still find ourselves doing the wrong things. Our thinking, though, is what determines our actions. Until we allow Jesus to change our hearts, minds, and attitudes, our actions will never be right.

You know, the unfortunate thing is that there are a lot of Christians out there who still don't know what the right actions are. They don't really know how to live a life that draws them closer to God every day, and that has a definite impact on the people around them.

It is important to spend time with God in prayer. If you don't spend time with him, there's no way you can know him. And if you don't know him, there's no way you can be like him.

Your presence is important also. You, and you alone, bring something into the corporate gathering of the church that nobody else can.

Giving is important because it's really just a willingness to give back some of what God has already given you.

Every single member should be plugged into some area of service in the church. At the church where I pastor, if you recall, we have a saying that "every member is a minister." That way, everybody shares the burden—and everybody shares in the joy of doing God's work and seeing his purposes come to pass both individually and corporately.

All of these are things that can be done with excellence, or they can be not done at all. The way I see it, you've come to a fork in the road, and you can either take the way that's right or the one that's left. As you travel, just remember that it's a process. You won't magically become like Jesus overnight, any more than a young boy goes to bed and wakes up a man. Sometimes you'll take two steps forward, and then you'll slide back a step. The most important thing is that we're headed the right direction. Where we're going is a whole lot more important than how fast we're getting there.

If we did all the things we are capable of doing, we would literally astound ourselves.
—Thomas Edison

It is a path that will eventually lead us to perfection. Along the way, though, the best we can aim for is excellence. The best we can do is our best. And the best promise we can receive is the one in Philippians 4:13, which tells us we can do all things through the One who gives us strength. We can be certain he'll give us the strength to do those things with excellence.

dive in
- *Where am I in my life on the way to becoming like Christ on a scale of one to ten?*
- *What is it about Jesus that makes him perfect?*
- *What kind of changes might God bring about in my life to make me more like Christ?*

chapter 40

claim your treasure

I came to church early one morning, and it was just me and our church administrator, Rusty. We walked into the sanctuary, and it was a little hot and stuffy. We realized that the air conditioner wasn't working properly.

I said, "Well, let's call the folks who can fix it, and get them out here." And he said, "No. I've learned how to start it." I responded, "You're kidding me," but apparently he wasn't.

He took me outside to the unit, and warned me not to get muddy. Then he picked up a stick and hit the thing—and it started. He said, "I'm not an engineer, but I know where to hit it."

Now, I could be wrong, but I'm going to guess that God has hit you in a spot or two recently. I don't mean I think he's picked up a stick and beat you with it. I think he's just put his finger on a place or two in your heart, the spots that can get you started, too. I say this because I know how God works. I know that if we're willing to put forth the effort and step out of the boat, that he'll meet us right where we are. And if you've been faithful to read, contemplate, and pray about all we've been learning for the last forty days, he's going to honor that commitment.

look ahead

It's come time, though, to look ahead, and ask ourselves what we're really going to do with all of this new understanding. It's time for us to develop a passion for the future.

There was once a man named Hezekiah, and the Bible tells us that he became king when he was twenty-five. And what a king he was. 2 Kings 18:3 says, "he did what was pleasing in the LORD's sight." Beyond that, according to verses 5–7:

> Hezekiah trusted in the LORD, the God of Israel. There was never another king like him in the land of Judah, either before or after his time. He remained faithful to the LORD in everything, and he carefully obeyed all the commands the LORD had given Moses. So the LORD was with him, and Hezekiah was successful in everything he did.

Eventually, though, Hezekiah became ill and was about to die, but he wasn't ready to go. In Isaiah 38:2, he wept bitterly, reminding God that he had always been faithful. God heard his prayers, and gave him another fifteen years. During that time, however, something happened to Hezekiah. He became proud and selfish. He began to trust in his own strength, rather than God's. He was warned that his short-sightedness would affect future generations, but he responded, "At least there will be peace and security during my lifetime" (Isaiah 39:8).

Do you know what happened next? As soon as he died, all of the good he had brought about died, too. The nation went right back to its sinful ways under the leadership of his son.

It's so easy for us to just focus on the right now, isn't it? As we see with Hezekiah, though, that can have disastrous results. When Hezekiah's son Manasseh took over, he actually reestablished some of the idolatrous practices that his father had worked so hard to destroy. He practiced sorcery, sacrificed his sons, and desecrated the Temple by putting idols in it. Things definitely went downhill.

> ## What is right is often forgotten by what is convenient.
>
> **—Bodie Thoene**

The warning is there for us, should we choose to see it. If we just focus on where we are right now, with no regard for what comes next, we'll quickly start going downhill, as well. Every day that we're not pressing toward becoming closer to Christ, we're falling further away.

learn from the past

Just as the last chapter of each part of this study reviewed the insights of the previous six days, we need to tip our hats to the past before we can fully move ahead. Tipping our hats helps us remember what's important. Remember what Moses said in Deuteronomy 6:10–12:

> The LORD your God will soon bring you into the land he swore to give your ancestors Abraham, Isaac, and Jacob. It is a land filled with large, prosperous cities that you did not build. The houses will be richly stocked with goods you did not produce. You will draw water from cisterns you did not dig, and you will eat from vineyards and olive trees you did not plant. When you have eaten your fill in this land, be careful not to forget the LORD, who rescued you from slavery in the land of Egypt.

At the time, he was talking to the Israelites, but it's just as relevant for us today. When we begin to enjoy all of the things that have come to us, we might be inclined to sit back and become complacent. It becomes easy to forget, but we don't want to do that.

Looking back also gives us an opportunity to learn. One day the disciples were complaining that they didn't have anything to eat. They forgot to bring bread, we're told in Mark 8, so there was only one loaf in the boat. (Keep in mind that this is after Jesus has miraculously fed the multitudes.) Jesus knew what they were thinking, so in verses 17–19, he said:

> Why are you so worried about having no food? Won't you ever learn or understand? Are your hearts too hard to take it in? You have eyes—can't you see? You have ears—can't you hear? Don't you remember anything at all? What about the five thousand men I fed with five loaves of bread? How many baskets of leftovers did you pick up afterward?

I would imagine they were a little sheepish in their response: "Twelve."

Jesus continued in verse 20, "And when I fed the four thousand with seven loaves, how many large baskets of leftovers did you pick up?" "Seven."

"Don't you understand even yet?"

Oh, that we could learn from the past. My own church was built on a spot that used to be an okra field. When folks came initially, they didn't have enough money to pay for things. I'm told they had meetings on Sunday nights when they would sit down and decide which bills could be paid that week. They raised and sold okra to help bring in some cash. That's the kind of dedication we can all learn from.

One other thing that happens when we look back is that we learn how to deal with our pride. It's not a case of "we deserve the things we have." Instead, we remember the people who came before, who laid the groundwork for us. On a personal level, we also realize the places where we used to be, and how—if it weren't for God—we might still be there. Just remember, as it's long been said, that the past is a good guidepost, but it's not meant to be a hitching post. We're not supposed to get stuck there.

get focused

Now is the time to roll up our sleeves, for us to remain focused on our priorities. That includes knowing God, but it also includes going out and making disciples. The church isn't here just so we can build buildings, and get together every so often and have a good time. We're here to bring people closer to Jesus. The great majority of people come to church initially because they're invited, not because of some program or advertising. It's our job, then, as members of the Body of Christ, to inspire them to come.

It's also our job to stay focused on unity. In Ephesians 4:3, Paul urged us, "Always keep yourselves united in the Holy Spirit, and bind yourselves together with peace." We're all on the same team. If you ask any coach, they'll tell you the same thing: If you want to win, there's nothing more important than unity. Remember, though, that unity isn't just a one-time thing. It has to be a daily decision. Just like making disciples. That's not something you do once, and then it's over. As for knowing God and lifting up Jesus, that's a constant process, too. All together, though, those daily decisions lead us to a glorious future.

> God wills that we should push on into His presence and live our whole life there.
>
> **—A. W. Tozer**

During the 2000 Olympics, the U.S. team was the one to beat in the women's 4x400 meter relay. They were considered a sure bet to win, but they didn't. Even though they were the best and the fastest, when it came to the final pass of the baton, they couldn't pull it off. One of the women dropped it.

You've got to know that there's no way you can win when you drop the baton. You can have all the promise in the world, but if you don't take what you've been given and pass it on to the next person in line, you're sure to lose.

In the grand scheme of things, all this isn't about your life. And it's not about mine, either. It's about passing the baton from one generation to the next. We can do that by being godly role models. Children and other people need to see others who are committed to Jesus, who are serving and not thinking of themselves. They need to see people who extend grace and forgiveness and love, who will help them out in their time of need. We have the opportunity to do that on both an individual level and a corporate one.

> **All that I have seen teaches me to trust the Creator for all I have not seen.**
>
> **—Ralph Waldo Emerson**

While we're at it, we need to make sure that we offer people limitless possibilities. It's unbelievable what God can do, and our faith can help open the doors for others, too. Are we the kind of people who hear the dreams people share, and encourage them on, no matter how big those dreams are? Or are we the kind to dampen enthusiasm and fill others with doubt? We can bless or we can curse; we can build up or we can tear down.

As we look ahead to a still uncertain future, there are things of which we can be certain. We can be certain that God loves us and that he'll never leave us. We can be certain that forgiveness is always there for the asking. We can also be certain that, as we humble ourselves before God, he will lift us up. It says so right there in James 4:10.

I dare you, then, to pray with confidence. I dare you to let God give you a new passion, to let it burn within you, for where he's leading you. The poorest man is not the man without a dollar, after all, but the man without a dream.

And if your dream is for a transformed life, one in which your spirit overflows with the goodness of God, you're going to get there. You're going to know the taste of that living water that satisfies your thirst like nothing else can.

dive in
- *What commitment am I ready to make to prayer?*
- *What commitment am I ready to make to presence?*
- *What commitment am I ready to make to gifts?*
- *What commitment am I ready to make to service?*

giving your life to Jesus

Some people think that all it takes to be a Christian is to go to church or to have been baptized as a baby. Attending worship services can certainly help get you on the right track, but there's another important step. You've got to accept Jesus as both Savior and Lord.

Doing so doesn't mean saying a bunch of magic words. Basically, it just means surrendering. Now, I know that the world teaches us that surrender is a bad thing. Some consider it a sign of weakness or defeat. But when it comes to being a Christian, it's actually a symbol of strength. It means you're aligning yourself with the greatest power in the universe, and you're willing to admit that you're not the one who's really in control. That's the "Lord" part.

As for the "Savior" part, that just means you admit that you've made mistakes in your life, and you'd like to be forgiven for them. See, we've all fallen short. Becoming a Christian, though, allows us to confess and essentially wipe the slate clean. God sent his son, Jesus, to take care of all those mistakes for us. He bore the brunt so we wouldn't have to.

If you don't remember ever confessing that Jesus is your Lord and Savior, you can take care of that, right now. Just repeat the prayer listed below. If it's your first time to do so, please let someone else know that you've done it. Tell a member of your church or a friend whom you know is a Christian. They'll help you take the next step.

> God, I know that I've made a lot of mistakes in my life. I know that I have sinned. But I believe that you can help wipe the slate clean. I believe you sent your son, Jesus, to die on the cross for me, and I accept him now as my Savior and Lord. God, I thank you for drawing me to you, I thank you for your forgiveness, and I thank you for the new life you have begun in me. I believe I am a new creation. Amen.

about the author

John Ed Mathison has been senior minister of Frazer Memorial United Methodist Church in Montgomery, Alabama, for thirty-four years. Under Mathison's leadership, Frazer has grown in membership from 400 to more than 8,600 members, making it one of the fastest-growing United Methodist congregations in America.

The son of a United Methodist minister, Mathison holds a bachelor of arts degree from Huntingdon College, a bachelor of divinity degree from Candler School of Theology, a master of theology degree from Princeton University, and a doctor of ministry degree from Candler.

Mathison is a nationally-known and sought-after speaker. He has served as platform speaker for the National Conference of Fellowship of Christian Athletes and the National Hi-Y Tri-Hi-Y Conference. He is also a seminar speaker at the Billy Graham Training Center and at conferences nationwide.

In 1978, he was selected Montgomery's Man of the Year, and in 1994, he was selected as National Clergyman of the Year by the Religious Heritage of America. In 2005, he received the Martin Luther King Jr. Religion Legacy Award from Alabama State University.

Mathison's previous books are *Tried and True, Every Member in Ministry, Fishing for Birds*, and *Extra Effort*. He can be heard weekly on Montgomery-area radio stations and is seen on the *Frazer Family Worship* television program on the INSP and FAM-NET cable network.

Mathison and his wife, Lynn, have four children, Vicki, Lauren, Clay, and Si, and nine grandchildren.